Narrative Research in Ministry

A Postmodern Research Approach

for Faith Communities

Narrative Research in Ministry

A Postmodern Research Approach

for Faith Communities

by

Carl Savage

and William Presnell

Drew University Doctor of Ministry Program

Wayne E. Oates Institute

Louisville, Kentucky

Originally published by the Indian University Press in 2006

This book may be ordered online at:
www.oates.org/bookstore/nrim

ISBN 978-1-892990-28-0

Book design by A. Christopher Hammon

Published by the Wayne E. Oates Institute

Louisville, Kentucky

Printed in the United States of America

To

The Drew Doctor of Ministry students

Whose work with this approach

contributed to its development

Contents

18 Rungs in the New Ladder of Learning

by Leonard Sweet

I know of no work like the one you are about to read. Its richness and rarity comes from an uncommon combination of the particular and the universal.

The particular is a laser-like focus on the Doctor of Ministry project and the authors' proposed shift from a problem-solving methodology to a conversation-starting, metaphor-exegeting, story-catching/storytelling, systems-thinking, preferred-futures approach, or what they call a postmodern narrative approach to ministry research.

The universal is a wide-angle view of the changes taking place in culture today and the need to reinvent the ways in which theological education delivers ideas, information, and best practices to the tens of thousands of religious leaders who have the closest day-to-day contact with people.

Here is my list of eighteen transformations that are changing the nature of how we prepare leaders for the church. Some of these are addressed directly in this book. Some are implied. Some the authors may not even agree with. But here is one attempt to put the reason why this book is needed into a wider cultural and theoretical context.

There are 18 rungs for a reason. In rabbinic thought, Jacob's ladder had 18 rungs, symbolizing the 18 blessings contained in the Amidah, a daily prayer, each line forming one rung and corresponding to the vertebra in the spinal column.

These 18 rungs form the ladder forward to the future, a ladder which connects the body to the head, by the way, with the mind unifying the whole as the bodily holy of holies.

#1 Ministers must become life-long learners. The top priority for every student is to learn how to learn, for a lifetime of learning.

Life-long learning is The Prime Directive of ordained ministry, and an imperative for every disciple (mathetes = learner) of Jesus.

The Doctor of Ministry degree offers connected learning that enables imaginative, innovative, and transformative experiences which overcome the current norm of pastoral isolation and the various obstacles to participating in peer engaged continuing education. Continuing education has been called not without reason one of the fastest-growing industries of the 21st century.[1]

#2 Theological education is more important than ever. The question is whether seminary education as we know it, whether at the masters or doctoral level, is still the best delivery system for theological education.

Theological educators need to face facts: Some of the most influential and successful pastors in the US today were never credentialed by any accrediting system (e.g. Jim Cymbala of Brooklyn Tabernacle, Bill Hybels

---

[1] So argues John Chambers of Cisco Systems. The Wall Street Journal reports that Market Data Retrieval surveyed 1028 accredited two-and-four year colleges. They found that 72% offered online courses in 1999. Some 34% offered an accredited distance learning program. "The Corporatization of Ongoing Education", Trend Letter, 19 (5 October 2000), 2.

of Willow Creek), just as some of the most successful business leaders (e.g. Bill Gates, Larry Ellison, Steve Jobs, Steven Spielberg) never finished college. One survey in the 90's revealed that the pastors of 75 out of the one hundred largest churches in USAmerica did not have seminary degrees.[2] Studies conducted by Hartford Seminary (CT) reveal that congregations pastored by seminary-trained leaders are less likely to deal openly with conflict, are far more likely to lack a sense of mission or purpose, and quickly feel threatened by changes in worship.

The ultimate credentialing is not "Do you have a degree? but "Can you do ministry?" Or in terms of the language of the emerging culture, how good a network portal are you? Can you provide direct hyperlinks to the divine?

***

> Andrew Higgins, who built landing craft in WWII, refused to hire graduates of engineering schools, even though there was a lot of detail and invention involved in making those boats. He believed that they only teach you what you can't do in engineering school. His engineers were all self-taught. He started off at the beginning of the way with 20 employees. By the middle of the way, he had 30,000 people working for him. He turned out 20,000- landing craft. Dwight D. Eisenhower told me, "Andrew Higgins won the war for us. He did it without engineers."
>
> —military historian Stephen Ambrose[3]

***

---

[2] Ralph L. Lewis and Gregg Lewis, Learning to Preach Like Jesus [Wheaton, ILL: Crossway Books, 1989], 46.

[3] As quoted in "A Pure Ambrosia," *Fast Company*, May 2001, 172.

#3 The new learning methodology of the emerging culture is Wiki. Wiki is another name for the open architecture that features connected learning and peer-to-peer (P2) learning. A wiki is a rapidly growing web-based collaboration tool that is not just based on add-ons, but on actual content improvement. Although wikis are similar to bulletin boards or Web logs in some respects, there are several main differences.

Often, wiki fans cite the "napkin example" to explain. Two people sit down at a table in a restaurant. One scribbles an idea on a napkin. The other modifies the idea on the napkin -changing the wording, adding new thoughts, drawing sketches or otherwise contributing new content.

A wiki is the shared napkin in cyberspace. Anyone who is authorized can go into the shared workspace and add, delete or edit content anywhere on the wiki's Web page. Unlike bulletin boards and blogs, users are not limited to changing their own posts or commenting on others' contributions. They can actually change the existing content, even to the point of modifying another person's posts.

A blog usually belongs to one person, and mistakes are set in stone on bulletin boards. But a wiki is a community forum, where history is dynamic. Wikis offer any number of people the chance to think aloud, comment and correct one another. For examples, see wikipedia, wiktionary, wikiletics, etc.

#4 The Web is the primary delivery system for learning and faith development. What the book was to the modern world, the web will be to the world that is forming. Theological education must get over its aversion to and misunderstanding of the Internet. The most anti-social technology ever invented was the book, not the web. Education already is the next killer app online, and just-in-time training is the greatest need of continuing education. The Web can connect the learning to the person when the questions start to be asked. Just-in-time learning, not semester-based, print-oriented, classroom-learning, is the educational model of the future.

#5 Our thinking about learning must be shaped by the influences of learning theorists like Dewey, Whitehead, Knowles, Senge, Schön (his work on the reflective practitioner), Perelman (his theories of just in time learning), and Louis Kentner (e.g. his dictum that "no teacher can put anything into a pupil which is not already there").

This comes together in both face-to-face learning and distance learning. I don't do "classroom teaching" in either sense of the term.

I don't teach. I organize learning and mentor learners.

I don't do classes. I organize learning courses. I study with my students, and their participant-observer status means they shape the course of study much like a river takes its course from what it encounters on the journey. The ultimate syllabus is the student anyway.

#6 Traditionalist theological education and the burgeoning number of teaching churches (or Learning Churches, as I prefer to call them) are largely not only not talking to one another; they live in parallel universes. Leaders of the future need new partnerships and linkages between seminaries, judicatories, local congregations and emerging ministries. We must do theological education and ministry formation together, not separately.

#7 High Impact Learning (HIL) experiences, such as the already hot 2-3 day conferencing phenomena, or what I prefer to call learning advances, will continue to catch fire even though their shape will become more relationship based and less sage-on-a-stage driven. Leaders naturally seek tribal gatherings of like minded souls to make new connections, learn new things, and immerse themselves in Socratic processes for a few intense days.[4]

#8 Leveraging change in existing theological schools and denominational accreditation processes has proven to be slim: mountains of money mostly give birth to mice. Nevertheless, the future is less about reforming existing credentialing systems than using what already exists to launch credible, new alternatives and supplements for missional and ministry development programs.

#9 The mission of ministerial education needs redefining. Thus the focus will not be on theological or ministerial education but on missional education, not on the certification of leadership for denominationally credentialed ministry but rather on the content and context requirements of missional ministry that can effectively build diverse bodies of Christ for this emerging culture. Theological education is too clerical in orientation and not sufficiently focused on the priesthood of believers.[5] It is too captivated by the heresy of clerisy.

#10 An action-reflection model is assumed for the future. The in-ministry model of Jesus and Paul needs to be rediscovered, or what some have called reflective practitioners. Paul didn't train anyone for ministry; he trained them in ministry. Ministry development should enable students to learn ministry in practice and not train them for practice. This is less a matter of seeing the relationship as

---

[4] Some call these conferences Free Agent Nation Clubs or F.A.N. Club meetings. See Daniel H. Pink, chapter on "School's Out" in *Free-Agent Nation* (Warner Books, 2001). ix

[5] See Ephesians 4:11-12.

theory to practice (a rational paradigm) and more as reflective-in-action or, if you insist, theory-in-practice. Theological education used to be a profession based on apprenticeship rather than scholarship.[6] If the local church is by design the most effective incubator of spiritual leaders on the planet,[7] then the education of the church's leader needs to revolve around what that leader spends the majority of his/her ministry attending to: the congregation.[8]

#11 The search for a new core curriculum for theological education is problematic because the whole concept of curriculum is problematic. Church leadership today requires a mentor plus action/reflection methodology in which the character, spiritual authenticity and missional passion of the mentor is more important than the curriculum. This is the new core around which some form of the old core curriculum in Bible, Patristics, Church History, Christology, Missiology, leadership/entrepreneurship, etc. will need to be recapitulated.

---

[6] Psychiatry still is. See T. M. Luhrmann, *Of Two Minds* (NY: Knopf, 2000).

[7] Rowland Forman, Jeff Jones, Bruce Miller, *The Leadership Baton* (Zondervan, 2004), 25.

[8] James F. Hopewell, Congregation: Stories and Structures (Augsburg Fortress, 1987). This is one reason Lyle Schaller calls for a multiple-track model of theological education: One track calls for the seminary graduate to join the staff of a teaching church for a three-to-ten year post-seminary apprenticeship. Another track calls for the college or university graduate to skip seminary and join the staff of a teaching church. That person may study traditional seminary courses via distance learning, as a part-time commuter, or by the professors coming to the church campus to teach. See Lyle Schaller, "How Does the Culture Impact the Church? The Call to Customize," Net Results, November/December 2000, 5, 3-7.

#12
We need to explore self-organizing, complex adaptive approaches to contextual learning where students can choose participation in a network of teaching churches and public/corporate sector opportunities across the globe along with web-based interaction for ongoing coaching. An open-source system trusts faculty mentors to guide learners to other faculty whose competencies and interests best suit that student's particular needs.

#13
Words that need to focus future discussions include: narrative, systems, strategic, missional, relational, incarnational, prophetic, contextual, culture-engaging, open-source. It is a waste of time to get bogged down in asking political questions like: Does seminary education help or hurt pastoral ministry? or Does training for ministry have to be formal theological education? or What's wrong with theological education as it now stands?[9]

#14
The Miseducation of the Church's Leaders is all too apparent in the pervasive problem of the 3Ms: money, mileage, marriage.[10] The traditional teaching model of seminaries requires a student to (a) travel to a specific location; (b) spend approximately 1500 to 1600 hours in a classroom (e.g. 3-4 years); (c) pay tuition amounting to at least $30,000; (d) turn in a specified number of

[9] This assertion is further vindicated in a series of Auburn Studies, specifically Elizabeth Lynn and Barbara G. Wheeler, "Missing Connections: Public Perceptions of Theological Education and Religious Leadership," *Auburn Studies*, No. 6 (September 1999), 1-16.

[10] See Reggie McNeal's chapter What About Seminary? In *Revolution in Leadership: Training Apostles for Tomorrow's Church* (Nashville: Abingdon, 1998), 119-29.

reports and papers; and (e) pass the required written examinations. The accumulation of knowledge does not lead to the formation of a person; the accumulation of courses does not lead to the formation of a preacher.

#15

The future is not primarily face-to-face learning from a Master-Teacher) but shoulder to shoulder learning between a Master Learner and an Apprentice Learner. Carl George says that ministry training looks like this:

1) I do, you watch, we talk

2) I do, you help, we talk.

3) You do, I help, we talk.

4) You do, I watch, we talk.

5) We each begin to train someone else.[11]

#16

We need to make the congregation into a learning organism: organize the congregation's learning around mission and ministry arts rather than teaching and programs.

#17

One's baptism is one's ordination into ministry and mission. Every baptized disciple has both a ministry to the body and a mission in the world.

#18

In the 21st century, WHO you studied with will be a more important question than WHERE you studied. The name-

---

[11] Carl George, *Nine Keys to Effective Small Group Leadership* (Mansfield, Pa: Kingdom, 1997), 19, 61.

brand used to be the school; the name-brand in the future is the name, the image, the mentor who can steer the spiritual formation of the person through forming a life shaped by biblical relationships, a passion for knowing God, and an indigenous expression of faith in a specific cultural context.

***

What President Abraham Lincoln said in his annual message to Congress (01 December 1862) serves as the call to arms for buildings these 18 rungs to the ladder of the future: "as our case is new, we must think anew, and act anew".

Or in the words of the entire quote from Abraham Lincoln:

> The dogmas of the quiet past are inadequate to the stormy present. The occasion is piled high with difficulty and we must rise with the occasion. As our case is new, so we must think anew, and act anew. We must disenthrall ourselves, and then we shall save our country.

Or save our seminaries.

Leonard Sweet

Drew University

Narrative Research in Ministry:

A Postmodern Research Approach for Faith Communities

This user-friendly manual, which has been used at Drew since 2003, truly meets a need in the Doctor of Ministry universe. The fruits and rewards of such a postmodern, narrative approach to real-world research are revealed in its experiential use. In short, this text represents a new way seeing, thinking and describing reality, and thus a new and re-imagined approach to studying and learning from faith communities.

The Theological School of Drew University has offered the Doctor of Ministry degree since 1973, and the Doctor of Ministry Program has used the Myers case-study method since 1993. This approach to the integration of theory and practice resulted in a Doctor of Ministry degree at Drew that was academically rigorous and yet open to innovations and new theories in delivering an educational experience in touch with the real world and the practical needs of ministerial leaders who, after all, are the real experts in the study of their congregations and communities of faith. A particular subjectivity on the part of the participant-observer was acknowledged: yet rational analysis was expected from the faculty and objectivity sought on the part of our students who dutifully used the standard categories of research questions, methodological assumptions, relevant theory, social analysis, and interpretative construction. What we noticed over the years was the increasing use of technology, narrative theology, family systems theory and image-based approaches to doctoral projects and theses—which called our traditional enterprise into question. Clearly, a cultural shift was taking place and a new and more appropriate methodological approach to congregational studies and community assessment was needed in the Drew Doctor of Ministry program.

Beginning in 1996, as the sixth director of the Drew Doctor of Ministry program, I sought to build on nearly twenty-five years of expected integration of theory and practice in Doctor of Ministry education, yet change the program with the needs of the times. My Dean at that time, Leonard Sweet, challenged me to "march off the map" and join him in "reinventing theological education for a new world. His successor, Dean Maxine Clarke Beach, also was able to "think outside the box" in order to shape and wisely manage the transformations that Drew was undergoing at the beginning of the 21 century. Together, we found creative means and methods to inform a future and preferred Church. What was needed, the Drew Doctor of Ministry team agreed, was a more open, narrative, organic, imaginative, participatory and experiential approach to the Doctor of Ministry project-thesis for a postmodern culture.

Dr. Carl Savage, Associate Director of the Drew Doctor of Ministry program, and Dr. William Presnell, former Associate Director and current Doctor of Ministry faculty advisor, went to work on writing what was first called a Postmodern Primer for Doctor of Ministry Students.

Carl is an archeologist, a biblical-historical scholar of early Christianity, and a pastor for over 20 years as well as being a native postmodern thinker. Bill is a marriage and family psychotherapist who has taught Bowen Systems Theory and narrative research methodology at Drew for many years. Together, they carefully worked out the psychosocial and postmodern theological implications of this approach for what I like to call "new-world research." After years of academic dialogue and writing, developmental testing and revision, and in response to student evaluations and input, a much-need resource is now available—*Narrative Research in Ministry: A Postmodern Research Approach for Faith Communities.*

We have used unpublished versions of this manual here at Drew since 2003 in our required Methods for Ministry course during Summer Term. Student response has been extremely positive. Many of them, after they graduated, contact us to say how it this approach transformed their ministry and leadership. We are grateful to our students, especially our Oklahoma cohort that includes several Native American Doctor of Ministry students, for their enthusiastic use and thoughtful critique of the narrative research approach. We are also grateful to Dr. Robert Duncan, Jr., a Drew alumnus and now President of Bacone College, and Chief Kelley Haney of the Seminole Indian tribe in Oklahoma, for wanting to publish the current version of the text through Indian University Press.

I want to commend this manual to the larger Doctor of Ministry universe, as well as to practical theologians who take the postmodern milieu seriously and desire a new, intellectually-profound and critically-nuanced approach to an old set of questions, namely: what's your problem in your ministry setting; how will you describe and contextualize it; what methods and tools will you use to better understand and respond to your contexts, and how will you design and implement an act of ministry to address the problem or issue you have named?

Narrative Research in Ministry poses similar questions but in a new way. What is methodologically distinctive about the Drew approach is 1) the way we try to take the postmodern culture seriously, 2) a willingness to change the traditional academic nomenclature to reveal new meanings, and 3) the courage to develop a thoroughly postmodern approach to practical research for ministry in a new world.

In many ways, a postmodern narrative approach to new-world research is virtually premodern--a 'back to the future' or 'ancient/future' approach to the mystery of life and vitality of ministry. This Narrative Research In Ministry book is your guide to a 'present future.'

Michael J. Christensen, Ph.D.

Director of the Doctor of Ministry Program,

Drew University May 2006

Acknowledgements

We want to thank the many who have labored with us to produce this book. It is a truly postmodern effort, a synergy of scholarship and practice. The book incorporates, through our personal filters, the ideas of those who have taught us along our journey together with feedback from our Doctor of Ministry students.

It is better because of the editorial talents and personal and collegial support of those around us. Therefore it is important to us to recognize those who helped us: Dr. Michael J. Christensen, Director of the Doctor of Ministry program at Drew University for his valuable input, encouragement, and suggestions—often heeded, always valued; Dr. Leonard Sweet, E. Stanley Jones Chair of Evangelism at Drew University, whose pioneering work in postmodern ministry informed and leavened ours; Jeff Wittung, Editorial Assistant, Ancient Christian Commentary on Scripture, who read and critiqued the early manuscript with an editor's careful eye; Dr. Rob Duncan, President of Bacone College and Drew Doctor of Ministry adjunct instructor, whose willingness to try our ideas at his own academic ministry site added richness and depth to our approach; Rob Duncan III of Indian University Press at Bacone College, who guided us through the publishing phase; and Dr. Dorothy McDougall, Doctor of Ministry director at the Toronto School of Theology, and Dr. A. Christopher Hammon of the Wayne E. Oates Institute, both of whom read the manuscript and helped us stretch our thinking.

Finally, we wish to say thanks to our families, who are always there for us. We are particularly grateful for the patience, timely conversations, and loving support extended to us by our spouses, Charleen Green and Nancy Presnell.

Carl Savage and William Presnell

May 31, 2006

Introduction

We are in a real sense, our stories. Who we are, what we think, and how we act are all shaped by the many large and small stories that make up the discourse embedded in our multi-sensory social experience. It is this postmodern understanding of identity and reality that has prompted the authors to fashion a new way of thinking about doing research in faith communities today, particularly through a Doctor of Ministry program. It is our belief that, in order for faith communities to define themselves and to know what to do in ministry, they must first understand the multiple stories which intersect with a given ministry situation in their specific context.

Via Negativa is the way we often identify ourselves. In other words, we know that we are *not this or not that* even if we cannot positively state what exactly we *are*. Our identities, individual or corporate, can only be pointed to by way of constructions or analogies, that is, through story. Yet, often, all that we can say is, "It is not this, but it is like this."

The identity of the Doctor of Ministry degree has evolved in much the same way. It, too, has a story that continues to shape the degree's embodiment in a variety of educational institutions. Created as a way to promote increasing competency and excellence in the practice of ministry, or as the ultimate credential in continuing education programs, or as a means to satisfy ecclesial demand for doctoral status, the degree has often had the academic Ph.D. as its model.

The Doctor of Ministry degree, however, is not a "mini Ph.D." A Ph.D. focuses on the academic study of a theoretical problem or intellectual tradition in a "pure" sense, with no immediate thought of applying this knowledge to a particular situation. The Doctor of Ministry degree and project-thesis is not a full-blown applied research project.

While some Doctor of Ministry projects have modeled themselves after case study and clinical analytical models, Doctor of Ministry students are not expected to be experts in sociological or psychological research. For this reason the Doctor of Ministry paper has sometimes been relegated to a "junior" status in the academic community—neither academically sophisticated, nor methodologically rigorous.

Further, the Ph.D. dissertation is envisioned as a broadening of knowledge on a given subject without emphasis on its practical ramifications. In contrast to this, the Doctor of Ministry thesis not only broadens knowledge of the ministry subject, but also reflects upon its applied practice.

So, if it is not a dissertation, and it is not a research paper, then what is it? William Myers has stated that "each author seeks to reflect critically on some facet of ministry and to communicate her/his reflections to her/his professional colleagues."[1] This has essentially been the defining criterion for evaluating Doctor of Ministry work for the past few decades. But notice its implicit focus: the Doctor of Ministry student is to be the expert evaluating and communicating to like experts in a professional field.

At the Drew University Theological School we have made a modification to this implicit focus for quite some time, long before our present project of re-imagining the Doctor of Ministry project-thesis. At Drew, since 1998, the student is expected to employ a lay-advisory team whose job is to inform, advise, and participate in the project. Likewise, the ministerial context (faith community) of the student is not simply the data field for study, but is expected to participate in the project. In other words, students are not simply doing critical reflection, but are engaged in ministry. The communication of reflections is not the goal of the paper. Mentoring, modeling, or motivating similar ministry changes and

---

[1] William Myers, *Research in Ministry: A Primer for the Doctor of Ministry Program, Studies in Ministry and Parish Life* (Chicago: Exploration Press, 2000), xv.

challenges in other ministry settings, not just to "professional colleagues," is the desired result of one's work.

Negatively, IT (the project-thesis) is not an academic exercise; it is pursued within the context of ministry. IT is not a research paper or case study, although it may inform ministry practice. IT is not a "professional paper" to discuss implications of self-discovery to other professionals. Positively, IT is a theological reflection and description of ministerial practice that represents the synergistic dialogue between various contexts of all those impacted by the process: social and cultural contexts; biblical, theological and denominational contexts; and personal contexts.

This book is both theoretical and practical. The reader is presented with the theoretical approach, and then walked through its application to an actual ministry situation. A sample project outline is constructed from preliminary research, demonstrating the movement from the study of narratives to a ministry project that interacts with the concern or opportunity uncovered in them. Critical thinking and theological reflection are exemplified. Means and methods for research are described and procedures for evaluation of ministries are explained.

Intended primarily as a text for student researchers in Doctor of Ministry programs, we feel that this book is a good introduction to the application of a narrative research approach to the study of the faith communities. These communities contain storied faith experiences, common practices, heartaches, conflicts, and potential for transformational ministry. While our students utilized this approach in the context of their academic pursuits, the use of the approach also proved useful within the contexts of their congregations beyond their academic work.

As in the past, church leaders today are vitally interested in theory and method for the study of congregations that are in line with the historical moment and the perceptions of reality that frame the intellectual landscape. To be relevant and energizing to future generations of believers, news of Word, Sacrament and Compassionate Ministry must be conveyed in language and thought forms appropriate to the emerging world. For us, here and now, this means engaging the defining metaphors and intellectual framework of postmodernity and placing them in the service of research for ministry. While a plethora of postmodern philosophical writings exists, there is a consensus around some tenets of this intellectual stance that give a fresh face and promising starting place for theological discussion and research methods for ministry. In this book we describe a new approach to the study of faith communities that is designed to move the leader/researcher in this direction.

CHAPTER 1

The New Approach

One cannot start, as I had been taught to do, by asking, if
you "agree with the doctrine." Rather, one must first work
back to the story, then to the dance, and finally begin to
glimpse the experience that lies behind these expressions.[1]

—Rosemary Radford Ruether

It is our intention in this book to respond to the realities of postmodernity
and the accompanying paradigmatic changes which now challenge
communities of faith. Out of our conviction that the reality experienced by
contemporary people is intentional, relational, and storied, we offer a new
pastoral narrative/theological hermeneutic and research approach that
departs from the research outlook and worldview of the modern era. We
are scholar-practitioners who draw from our extensive background in
social science and ministry practice. We offer a fresh approach which
engages the postmodern realities, including the conviction that all research
methodological traditions are merely competing stories which intersect
with many others that affect a given ministry in a given place and time.
Believing that all theology is descriptive theology and that only
contextually grounded theological statements are reliable guides for the
practitioner, we craft a postmodern multi-sensual narrative hermeneutic
which integrates narrative biblical theology (Frei and Barnes) with
narrative family therapy methodology (Freedman and Combs, Epston). In

---

[1] Rosemary Radford Ruether, *Disputed Questions: On Being a Christian,
Journeys in Faith* (Nashville: Abingdon, 1982), 27.

so doing, we hope to provide a procedural map for studying and reflecting upon the multiple, intersecting stories surrounding a narrative of concern in ministry. Our map is drawn as an interpretive narrative matrix in which reside the personal and faith stories of the researcher, the intersecting stories of the faith community's praxis, their religious traditions, and research stories garnered from readings, found documents, contextual study (demographics, culture, other social science research, history, etc.) and the study of symbol, ritual, and artifacts.

A basic primer for Doctor of Ministry project-theses has been a book by Myers entitled *Research in Ministry: A Primer for the Doctor of Ministry Program.*[2] In fact, we cite it in the previous version of our Drew Doctor of Ministry Handbook as the source to determine how Doctor of Ministry project theses are to be written. However, what was once at the breaking edge of the culture has now become submerged in newer developments. The Drew Doctor of Ministry has now evolved beyond this model. Myers' pioneer work crystallized a view of the Doctor of Ministry degree that was formulated in what we now call "old paradigm" thinking—intellectual thinking that was formed and shaped by a world view now known as Modernism. Modernism as the pervasive mode and approach to sociology, science, and theology peaked perhaps in the 1950's and 60's, but true to form from previous eras, theological studies often are the last bastions of old paradigm thinking. Scientists and sociologists have already moved beyond the reductionism of modernity. Generally, Modernism focused on discovering cause and effect and examining component pieces—like a child taking apart toys in "exploratory engineering."

---

[2] Myers, *Research in Ministry: A Primer for the Doctor of Ministry Program, Studies in Ministry and Parish Life* (Chicago: Exploration Press, 2000).

Theological studies may yet be engaged in such activity. Thus, the impact and synergy of newer insights from cognate fields may go unnoticed in our sphere of interest for some time.

Our new approach seeks to enable Doctor of Ministry students to employ what are often strengths in pastoral work—the ability to engage in story and the network of relationships with their ministry setting. This approach removes the embedded assumption in modern research that "hard data" are to be prioritized over "soft data." It also recognizes that in work with persons, the components of identity formation are not necessarily consistently held. People and groups will often hold a portrait of their own self that cannot be sustained when viewed from other perspectives. This picture of their identity can be either over or under-inflated, and often both at the same time. Their notion of the "what is" can be based on false assumptions of the past and/or self-limited projections of the future.

The new approach we are introducing is a process by which to uncover the present in its grasped state by gathering many data stories about a given ministry context. These stories are not just derived from anecdotal ethnographic listening, but include many research methods. The multiplicity of perspective gained from such a framework will enable the appreciation and apprehension of meaning and relationship patterns within the context and their connection to the larger human story and within the setting in the story of God's interaction with creation.

We begin exploring this new approach by examining what we wish to glean from postmodernity.

Postmodernism: What It Is and What It Is Not

Postmodern sociology and postmodern science, if there are things to be called such, now explore networks and functionalities seeking to understand patterns in complexity. They are pursuing questions of why things are the way they are from perspectives not based in a grinding reductionism. The whole is now seen as something that cannot simply be explained from a mere detailing, analysis, and summation of the parts. There is a linkage, network, and interaction that also must be explored. From chaos and complexity, patterns of spontaneous order sometimes appear. And systems—whether digital, biological or societal—exhibit identical characteristics hitherto unnoticed. It is this new orientation that informs our own new approach.

Postmodernity appears to have two parents: one creative and the other reactive. The one parent is a new creative look at the connectivity of all things. The other is a reaction to the perceived failures of the modern worldview. Postmodernism is thus the illusive child of creative and reactive modernities. However, knowing the parents is not the same as knowing the child.

Postmodernism:

It . . . comes out of literary critical deconstructionism.

It . . . arises from the failure of the modern vision of technological utopia.

It . . . develops from "those dwelling in the dregs of modernity, preoccupied by the shutdown of sustainable ecologies, viable communities, and historical hopes."[3]

It is a new description/perception of what we experience as reality.

It is marked with certain characteristics. Leonard Sweet alludes to several of these in his book, *Eleven Genetic Gateways to Spiritual Awakening*: "For quite some time I have been arguing that 'the postmodernist always rings twice'; that in postmodern culture, we must (in a 'both/and' rather than 'either/or' fashion) get more ancient and more future at the same time. This book is my attempt to work out this ancient/future methodology in the context of my own tribe."[4] "Both/and,"

---

[3] Catherine Keller, *Apocalypse Now and Then: A Feminist Guide to the End of the World* (Boston: Beacon Press, 1996), 2.

[4] Leonard I. Sweet, *Eleven Genetic Gateways to Spiritual Awakening* (Nashville: Abingdon, 1998), 15.

"ancient/future," "my own tribe"—these are all part of the postmodern constellation of understanding the world.

It is what modernism is not. Or, rather, it is characterized not by a buoyant optimism, but a constructive ambivalence at best, or a pervading pessimism at worst.

It is not so much the next phase of history—because it has a lot to say that negates history as defined by modernism—as it is an alternative perspective already residing in the last years of modernism. "Postmodernism therefore does not come after; but with modernism."[5]

Stanley Grenz uses the word "bricolage" when describing postmodernism. "Bricolage" is defined as "the reconfiguration of various traditional objects (typically elements from previous stages in the tradition of the artistic medium) in order to achieve some contemporary purpose or make an ironic statement."[6] He uses it to explain the nature of the diversity that is celebrated in postmodernism. It is, in a sense, more than eclectic. It is synergistic. Within postmodernity, all things may be considered equally valid so previously unrelated things may be employed to create a new whole. Previous context is unnecessary to meaning; meaning comes from the new context. You as postmodernist create the narrative. You do not simply read a script. A script would indicate a required structure, plan, or framework imposed from outside the emerging story.

How else may we describe postmodernity?

What is it? What is it not? What is it like?

Perceptions

Postmodernity can be said to have its infancy in the television age (1950-60), the age which began to globalize society beyond all previous

---

[5] Keller, *Apocalypse*, 289.

[6] Stanley Grenz, *A Primer on Postmodernism* (Grand Rapids, MI: Eerdmans, 1996), 21.

eras. No longer was the local community the center of the universe. As Stanley Grenz points out, centerlessness is characteristic of postmodernism.

This is a particular sort of centerlessness: one that blurs spatial and temporal distinctions—merging past, present and envisioned future, along with local and distant—every place and time arrives into your place via the same conduit. Onto the screen, once TV and now computer, comes the collage of images that embody the "objective world." It is the filter that blends space and time into an "ever-present." The postmodern narrative vision is that there are no boundaries between past and present, and only vague borders between objective and subjective. Even now it has become difficult to distinguish between the computer generated and digitally photographed, take for example the movies in the *Lord of the Rings* trilogy where the character Golum is a type of animated hybrid. This blurriness is why the postmodernists remain unsure that any of our perceptions are ever more focused. They are also skeptical of the presentation of information by traditional sources. All "facts" are merely the selected data and propaganda reflecting the perspective of the reporter, and inevitably are selected with a political agenda, however covert or innocent. Postmodernism privileges the present moment and chooses primordial perceptions as alternative to modern space-time categories. One could think of it as a sacrament of the present moment.

In my (Carl's) first undergraduate sociology course on methods, our first reading assignment was the book *How to Lie with Statistics*.[7] The book illustrates how we are constantly bombarded with information colored with a message, and are most aware of this only when it is in the form of commercial advertising or political propaganda. Ever listen to the old Soviet Union shortwave radio station broadcasting the "news"? It was one of the strongest on the shortwave bands. The information it transmitted, however, was very different from our local media. But for the postmodernist, those cases are merely indicative of the subtle process that

---

[7] Darrell Huff, *How to Lie with Statistics* (New York: Norton, 1954).

occurs with all transmission of information or tradition. Nothing is truly neutral, everything is biased. Postmodern skepticism is mirrored in the TV show *X-files*: The Truth is Out There . . . but Trust No One.

Further, this notion of the power of language and story is pervasive. The February 2003 issue of *Prevention* magazine contained one of the most concise definitions of this power that we have seen. In a sidebar entitled *The Power of Language and Stories* was found the following:

> We don't describe the world we see; we see the world we
> describe. Language has the power to alter perception. We
> think in words. These words have the power to limit us or to
> set us free; they can frighten us or evoke courage. Similarly,
> the stories we tell ourselves about our own life eventually
> become our life. We can tell healthy stories or horror
> stories. The choice is ours.[8]

The postmodern spirit may first hear sounds and see images, and then connects the dots. We tell stories. Telling stories, we use words, metaphors, and motifs, etc.; we conceptualize these into abstractions.

The Change in Perception

The premodern affirmation was Anselm's "I believe in order that I may understand." The modern affirmation was embodied in "I believe what I can understand."[9] The postmodern affirmation is? (Understanding is not belief.) "What will happen if I believe this?" or "What does it do to my world if I believe this?"

Let's look at several ways at seeing how the postmodern perception differs from the modern worldview. Each of these in their way reflects the

---

[8] "The Power of Language and Stories," *Prevention* 55 (February 2003): 139.

[9] Grenz, *Primer on Postmodernism*, 62.

concept of centerlessness. Textually we have to present these linearly, but priority in text does not indicate priority for understanding. Think of the movie *Pulp Fiction*:

> The film tells interlocking stories, which unfold out of
> chronological order, so that the movie's ending hooks up
> with the beginning, most of its middle happens after the
> ending, and a major character is on screen after he has been
> shot dead. Why is the movie told in this way? For three
> reasons, perhaps: (1) Because Q.T., as his fans call him, is
> tired of linear plots that slog wearily from A to Z; (2) to
> make the script reveal itself like "hypertext," in which
> "buttons" like the gold watch or "foot massage" lead to
> payoffs like Butch's story or Vincent's date from hell; and
> (3) because each of the main stories ends with some form of
> redemption. The key redemption—the decision by Jules
> (Samuel L. Jackson) to retire from crime after his life is
> saved by a "miracle"—is properly placed at the end of the
> file even though it doesn't happen at the end of the story.[10]

If you've seen it, at what point did you realize that what you saw first was the result of everything that followed rather than vice-versa? Your movie present was the working out of the future, and priority was given to meaning—constructed, not inherent—not chronology . . . a very postmodern composition.

The Past (or Future) Ain't What It Used to Be

Grenz points out a crucial postulate of postmodernism: the present is not the inevitable working out of the past.[11] In fact it seeks to show that

---

[10] Roger Ebert, "Secrets of *Pulp Fiction*," 1995, www.godamongdirectors.com/tarantino/faq/secrets.html.

[11] Grenz, *Primer on Postmodernism*, 136.

there is actually more discontinuity than continuity—that continuity is a "myth," only a modern historical construct that dissolves and blurs the uniqueness of singular events. We are left with sink holes of discontinuity.

The concept of "history" is therefore suspect as a paradigm and is flawed by its pursuit of the fundamental errors of Western society, which are said to be:

1. That an objective body of knowledge exists.

2. That such knowledge is possessed and is neutral or value-free.

3. That the pursuit of such knowledge benefits all humanity and not just a specific class.[12]

Because of this, Foucault, one of the "founders" of postmodernism, speaks of genealogy instead of history. History supposedly narrates the story of what really happened, to explain events accurately. Genealogy is supposed to give an idea of how the present came to be by tracing how a concept or discipline was constructed from previous conditions and political climates. Postmodern approaches to both of these disciplines suggest that both record the perspective of the presenter/story teller. Further, genealogy can be said to create the present or change the present by selecting data and explaining the past in new ways. Genealogy is really "a method for analyzing established theories in terms of their effects,"[13] and effectiveness has value for postmodernism. Genealogy is the telling of the discourse that makes or unmakes our world. For the postmodernists there is no "natural order," for that is just an invention. The present is "birthed" by the past and is not simply a result of cause or consequence.[14] The appropriate metaphor is organic, not mechanical. The present is not programmed by the cogs or code of causal determination; it freely responds to many stimuli of interpretation.

---

[12] Grenz, *Primer on Postmodernism*, 131.

[13] Grenz, *Primer on Postmodernism*, 136. 21

[14] Michel. Foucault, "Nietzsche, Genealogy, History," in *Language, Counter-Memory, Practice Selected Essays and Interviews* (Ithaca, N.Y.: Cornell University Press, 1977), 145.

So what we speak about has no underlying ontological validity as in some modern theories of language, which hold that language recognizes itself in a corresponding relationship with the world.

What does this all mean in our present context and climate? The "order of things" is simply the result of selective "readings" and interpretations of the past. The way things are is not the way they have/had to be/become.

We can go farther. Derrida, another postmodern "founder," leads us to this conclusion: the refutation of the notion of a singular meaning of a text, situation, or reality. [15] Every text is fluid—no fixed origin, identity, or end. Each act of reading is a preface to the next interpretation, which is why dialogue with the text is necessary.

"Text" can have the dual meaning of literary creation and societal structure. The way we say things are depends on our context, our "tribe." The way we say things are is not the only way they are: "each description would actually alter and color the experience itself . . . depending on circumstances."[16] So our present is not simply the next in the progression of other presents—linear history—our present is our interpretation conditioned by means of our conceptual system, our ahistorical truth system.

One of the lessons remembered from a course in exegesis of Isaiah taught by Dr. Dewey Beegle has to do with this concept of ahistorical truth. Although he did not use the term, he expected one to find the "timeless" truths out of an investigation of the historical-cultural milieu of each prophecy. One was to find the universal lesson circumscribed in the historical context.

Central to postmodern perception is that there are no universals. There is a parallel sense that truths can be separated ahistorically from a cultural context. This is a kind of phenomenological approach to truth. In a

---

[15] Grenz, *Primer on Postmodernism*, 146.

[16] Grenz, *Primer on Postmodernism*, 144. 23

way it also mirrors the approach one finds in the rabbinic literature. The Talmud is not so much an historical record of the development of Rabbinic thought as it is an explication of their phenomenological derivation of the true interpretation of scripture. It develops in the current community's appropriation of the past . . . selectively.

In the postmodern contextualization, therefore, we should now discover in conversation with others whereas previously we only explored the universe scientifically and historically. Ever notice how on Star Trek (any version) they really do very little science? Everything is meeting the new in their selves or in the "alien." The discoveries come in learning new interpretations, not necessarily new knowledge.

While there may be no agreement on universal stories or "truth" (meta-narratives), there may be agreement on the universal condition—we are in this together. There exists a universal interconnectedness. And so, instead of seeking individual self-sufficiency or salvation per se, one seeks meaning and wholeness in community and relationships. God may be manifest in the universal inter-connectedness of all things.

We are now unmoored from a single tether to ultimate reality. But is this leading us to a dangerous relativism? Are all communities of interpretation equal? The goal of postmodernism is unforced agreement blended with tolerant disagreement.[17] But one suspects the goal, measured by postmodern effectiveness, may be just as oppressive as the modernistic goal of unified knowledge.

We come to a second list. This list, like the first, is not inclusive of all that is postmodernism. A list, of course, is a modern approach to understanding what a thing signifies. In a truly postmodern sense something can only be understood when actualized, experienced, or used as a basis for further identity, but here is a list that may characterize postmodernity:

❖ skepticism of information sources

❖ critical suspicion of authority

---

[17] Grenz, *Primer on Postmodernism*, 159.

- ❖ the non-inevitability of the past/present/future

- ❖ ahistorical non-universal truths

- ❖ contextualization—things are known only through and relative to the social context

- ❖ centerlessness—or perhaps a better word is "de-centered", there is no ultimate reality at the center of existence, only the web of interrelatedness

Community is the locus of meaning in the postmodern sense. It provides the context of experience, which is the framework that interprets. What "tribe" we belong to influences everything, although "tribe" need no longer be thought of in terms of geographical location. The internet makes distance/proximity, youth/aged, male/female, majority/minority archaic distinctions—there is no longer Jew or Greek, there is no longer slave or free, there is no longer male or female (sound familiar? Although here not in Christ but in the anonymity of cyberspace.) One is free to find interpersonal connection of a kind and to create a constructed self. But is that true community?

Where have we in the church been told of community? And is it in reality present in our church?

Rodney Stark in his book *The Rise of Christianity* makes an interesting observation concerning the origins of movements. Working from his primary background of sociology, Stark points out that:

> the origins of ideas and of movements need not and often are not, the same. Consider the many modern groups with spurious claims to unbroken descent from ancient pagan cults. Judged by their doctrines, their claims to be of ancient origin are true. But an examination of their "human history" reveals them to be of contemporary origins.[18]

---

[18] Rodney Stark, *The Rise of Christianity: A Sociologist Reconsiders History* (Princeton, NJ: Princeton University Press, 1996), 142–43.

Stark suggests that Christianity grew primarily on the basis of its community and not primarily because of its ideas:

> the claim that mass conversions to Christianity took place as crowds spontaneously responded to evangelists assumes that doctrinal appeal lies at the heart of the conversion process. . . . But modern social science relegates doctrinal appeal to a very secondary role, claiming that most people do not really become very attached to the doctrines of their new faith until after their conversion.[19]

Thus, Stark indicates that the coalescent force of ideas would be a weak force in the face of other factors. The primary factor to effect conversion is "bringing one's religious behavior into alignment with that of one's friends and family members,"[20] or, in the language we have been using here, into alignment with one's effective community. Ideas rarely convert, interconnecting relationships transform. Community is the locus. The biblical story of Ruth is an example of this notion. Read it again. What is the progression to faith? You, your people, your god becomes myself, my people, my God, doesn't it? "And Ruth said, 'Entreat me not to leave you, or to return from following after you: for where you go, I will go; and where you lodge, I will lodge: your people shall be my people, and you God my God'" (Ruth 1:16).

Postmodernity and the Narrative Metaphor

A plunge into postmodern thinking means unloading some of the cherished notions of Western social science. In contrast to the modernist position that knowledge is objective, postmoderns are beginning to frame culture in terms of that which we ourselves socially "construct." Human cultures, in this view, are a function of human experience, are externalized

---

[19] Stark, *Rise of Christianity*, 14–15.

[20] Stark, *Rise of Christianity*, 17

to appear imposed rather than built, and are then given some divine or philosophical endorsement. This process of externalizing social reality has been termed "reification" or "the apprehension of the products of human activity as if they were something else than human products" by sociologist Peter L. Berger.[21]

Paradigm shifts within science also shed new light on the contrast between modernism and postmodernism. Scientific discoveries are important, according to Thomas Kuhn, because they reflect the fact that the scientist "sees differently":

> In learning to see oxygen . . . Lavoisier also had to change his view of many other more familiar substances. He had, for example, to see a compound ore where Priestley and his contemporaries had seen an elementary earth. . . . At the very least, as a result of discovering oxygen, Lavoisier saw nature differently. And in the absence of some recourse to that hypothetical fixed nature that he "saw differently," the principle of economy will urge us to say that after discovering oxygen Lavoisier worked in a different world.[22]

In other words, postmodern scientists have discovered that we do not live in a world of "mere facts," but interpreted data. The question concerning scientific observation may have changed: "Is it true?" ("Does it match reality?") may be supplanted by "In what way is it useful?" ("Does it bring more understanding?"). It is a shift from objective knowledge to

---

[21] Peter L. Berger and Thomas Luckman, "The Dehumanized World," in *The Truth About the Truth: De-Confusing and Re-Constructing the Postmodern World*, ed. Walt Anderson, A New Consciousness Reader (New York: Putnam, 1995), 36. Thanks to Dr. James Beebe for alerting us to this reference.

[22] Thomas Kuhn, "Scientists and Their Worldview," in *The Truth About the Truth: De-Confusing and Re-Constructing the Postmodern World*, ed. Walt Anderson, A New Consciousness Reader (New York: Putnam, 1995), 195. Thanks to Dr. James Beebe for alerting us to this reference.

functional information. Further, in a postmodern approach to connecting around shared observation and experience, the leader/researcher keeps in mind that functional meanings discovered in the relatedness of all things, including human relationships, are organized and communicated in story form. "To be human is above all to have a story."[23] This statement relates the way that many narrative theologians describe a general theory of human experience. However, the starting point for these theologians is the "scriptural story" rather than a theory of narrative, and an understanding that all theology is narrative theology. Paul Ricoeur states that narrative renders experience significant and humanly meaningful.[24] The narrative configures the multiplicity, discordance and succession of experience into story. Otherwise experience is just "one damn thing after another."[25] Narrative is configurative coalescence of one story out of many. It distinguishes character, action and circumstance so that one can decide whether an occurrence is an incident or an event, has intention or was accidental. It creates or demonstrates *kairos* out of *chronos*—a sense of being of or in time.

Re-imagining the process of configuration can change the future that is intended or directed from a recounted narrative. A story intends a future. It contains recognition of what has happened and possibility of what is to come. While history is supposedly aimed at the past, narrative is aimed at a tradition. Narrative's aim is to express meaning (myth-making— gathering meaning into a story that organizes and expresses part of a tradition and its practices) and to address the presently held order (parable-telling—comparing things from the spiritual realm to things in ordinary

---

[23] Hans W. Frei, *Theology and Narrative: Selected Essays*, ed. William C. Placher and George Hunsinger (New York: Oxford University Press, 1993), 208.

[24] Paul Ricœr, *Time and Narrative* (Chicago: University of Chicago Press, 1984), 3.

[25] To recontextualize Elbert Hubbard's quote somewhat: "Life is just one damned thing after another." Elbert Hubbard (1856–1915), U.S. author. The Philistine (Dec. 1909).

life for a teaching purpose). There is no knowing in a neutral fashion. Story, not past, renders identity. To be baptized is not indoctrination, but to be absorbed into the story of the Tradition.

But how does one assess whether or not the signified new narrative is an appropriate thing? Postmodern thinkers see all reality, including personal identity, as always "under construction"—a social construction of reality—and personal identity is seen therefore as a fluid composite of a number of "subject positions" the person occupies in the social order. People assume a varied number of identities, each contingent upon a position. Each position engages the person in a particular social discourse, or conversation (narrative) laden with values, norms, and power alignments. Discourses are organized ways of behaving that provide frameworks for making sense of the world. Personal power is dependent upon one's position in the discourse. These conversations shape a life story.

Reality is intentional, relational and storied. Yet, how does one assess the "realness" or "rightness" of a story that is held as normative? Tied up in the answer to this question is the notion of discernment. That is, we are not suggesting that we apply a standard of functionality to a story and *measure* it against such a rule. Such a measuring might impose structure. Discernment, rather, is a process, a participatory process, wherein one actively engages the story to sense its fit for "a healthy lifestyle" or "a preferred future." By discerning and not measuring we hope to avoid the language of pathology: a language in which difference is labeled "wrongness."

An example from my personal history (Carl) that illustrates a move in the medical community from treating conditions to treating patients, may illustrate the process of discernment. It illustrates a movement from measuring against a standard treatment of a condition to one of discerning the preferred future from the "what is."

I tore cartilage in my knee playing soccer as a "mature" adult. The orthopedic surgeon who treated my condition wrote a note to my family physician stating that, because of the condition of my knees, my soccer career was over and that I should pursue alternate activities. He had treated the condition. My family physician, knowing more of my background, history, interests and more general health, gave different advice. He noted that the health benefits derived from pursuing a recreation that I enjoyed outweighed the conservative position of ending the activity, *for me*. He, of course, added other admonitions: including better conditioning, strengthening the surrounding muscles, and being aware that if there were continued pain after rehabilitation that would truly be sign that I couldn't continue. He made this assessment based on the fact that benefits to my health outweighed the standard treatment. I continued to play soccer for another ten years.

In the measuring model, exemplified by the stance of the orthopedic surgeon described above, any difference from a presumed standard would indicate divergence from the "truth." For example, science matches theory against observation. When there is congruence, one pre-supposes that the theory is "true" because it matches observed "reality." When there remain inconsistencies, either the theory is presumed false, or the observations are judged to be flawed. There is pathology present. That is to say, observation renders the theory abnormal, or untrue, since it is deemed outside of what is a commonly accepted standard.

But in the postmodern context that method is itself problematic. Scientific theory is, in the postmodern context, really just a story and observations are story-laden to begin with. There is no objective matching to reality, to the way things "really are." How can there be a true, overarching story when there are only competing stories? We can only match stories against one another. Political power may influence which of the competing story dominates, or the stories may remain isolated in their particularities.

Hence, instead of measuring, we need to discern. We look for the elegant story that simplifies understanding and incorporates difference and diversity. Instead of identifying pathologies we seek to discern the directions of harmony and function. We seek to uncover "realness" and "rightness." But how?

The concepts of realness and rightness are themselves the product of consensual social recognition and the socialization process. They reflect congruence with preferred conditions of being. Yet we can proceed to discern in the following suggested ways. These are not ways to discern, but questions to ask when attempting to practice discernment:

1. Is there a "plain sense" or a "coded sense" to the story?

2. Is the meaning intuitively self apparent/transparent or must it be interpreted?

3. Is the interpretation based in socialization or intuition?

Plain sense is not the same as literal sense. Plain sense reflects historic usage and common understanding of wider community. For example, "And if your right hand causes you to sin, cut it off and throw it away. It is better for you to lose one part of your body than for your whole body to go into hell" (Matthew 5:30). The literal sense requires physical violence and disfigurement, the plain sense understands the apparent metaphor. The more broad the group is that shares the "common sense" of the story the more plain the sense is. A coded story is one that needs an interpretative key to be given as esoteric teaching, the inside joke as opposed to the pangenic aphorism.

We begin with a sense that in Judeo-Christian tradition, truth has never been a matter of matching stories against reality. One begins with the story that is given to us. It is "revealed reality." In the Christian church, as G. Loughlin puts it, "a life-story . . . comes first,"[26] namely, the story of Jesus Christ. Our concepts of "realness" and "rightness" in this vein assume also a potential of faithfulness. They include a prominence of love, justice and care of creation. A "real" story has a transparency that the transcendent, that which transcends "what is" to "what is preferred to be," can be seen through it. It intends a future.

---

[26] Gerard Loughlin, *Telling God's Story: Bible, Church, and Narrative Theology* (New York: Cambridge University Press, 1996), 23.

A New Approach to Ministry in a Postmodern Context

What we are suggesting in this book is a new approach to effective ministry in the postmodern context. It includes, though it does not begin with, the issues of how that context is different than those that precede or proceed from the "what is." What is hoped is that this approach will make available to the leader/researcher a window into reality. We live in a structure that we are or are not comfortable with, a building that is partly imposed upon us and partly created by us. It is a dynamic structure that unfolds, evolves, changes. It is partly comprised of our words and actions and partly changes our neural pathways. It incorporates the definitive notion that our self, our community, our world is relational and storied. From our building we can open a window to the story—each window allowing in the freshness of an intersecting narrative. These intersecting narratives may be operative among different layers of interconnectedness. These layers form in the individual, the family, the church community, the judicatory, the denomination, the Tradition, and so on.

Our approach to ministry, then, requires that we have a layered portrait of our ministerial context. We are trying to grasp the "what is," the present in that context, and to understand how that moment is defined by its past and/or its future. We seek to catalog the present futures, the possible futures that are emerging and perhaps even then to encourage and enable a preferred future to prevail.

We frame all research methods that will enable our portrait to resolve itself as a collection of stories. There is no prioritization of "hard data" over "anecdotal data." We are trying to glimpse the unfolding of unique meaning from the interpersonal interaction we observe. We are not comparing the ongoing discourses to a normative script that infers a prior plan or framework, but we are trying to evoke the story so that we may hear its nuances and emergent meanings. We want our research methods to be evocative not prescriptive.

As we open windows to reality we expect to experience multi-sensory input from outside our location within the larger story. We expect to "hear" content and process. We expect to "smell" odors and fragrances that the story suggests or images. We expect to "taste" the food and hospitality of the ministerial context, to "feel" tension, stagnation, peace, textures—rough, stiff, rugged, smooth—exhibited in the contours of the narratives of the context. We expect to "see" the symbolic structures, gestures, rituals and relationship patterns.

Just as in archaeology, where one works from a very limited number of artifacts to reconstruct what was, so we with this approach are often trying to discern "what is" from a small sampling of the stories impinging upon our ministry context. In archaeology one often extrapolates on the basis of three or four aligned stones to portray a building or floor or wall. Likewise with this method we make assessments from the snippets we uncover about what the "what is" could be.

Elizabeth Barnes[27] has offered us one hermeneutical method which slides in nicely to this approach to congregational study. She agrees that story is primary to understanding the experience of people in relationship to each other and God. She also says that this storied tradition of the Christian faith is present in the church today, even though modern people may have only vague or incomplete connection with it. The way in which we can reestablish this connection in counsel and spiritual guidance, says Barnes, is to evoke the human story, and then mediate the interlacing of the biblical story with the human stories. Barnes continues:

> [B]iblical stories are normative precisely because they
> interlace with our other stories in a way that makes the
> biblical texts authoritatively functional as shapers of us
> and our view of the world. It is in this way that Christians

---

[27] Elizabeth B. Barnes, *The Story of Discipleship: Christ, Humanity, and Church in Narrative Perspective* (Nashville: Abingdon, 1995). Drawing on a variety of sources, including contemporary fiction, Barnes provides a creative and persuasive argument as to how narrative can enrich the church's understanding of the gospel.

can speak of the Bible as God's word and as God's living
Word. Scripture's liveliness inheres in its interlacing
genius. The power of the Spirit is the power to interlace
the biblical narratives with humankind's multitudinous
narratives so that transformation occurs and a true story is
told.[28]

By entangling the various stories of the contexts that we connect to
the larger stories of the faith traditions, including biblical stories, and
ultimately to God's story in the Word which forms us anew, we hope to
become more closely adjusted to and formed by God's story in the world.

---

[28] Barnes, *Story of Discipleship*, 9.

CHAPTER 2

Theological Reflection In Ministry Research

> Our understanding of a text is often far greater than our understanding of how we can understand it.
>
> —Hans Frei [1]

Introduction

In order to keep faith with our religious identity and the purposes of ministry, research in ministry must first be framed theologically. That is the starting block for the Doctor of Ministry project-thesis at Drew. Ministry situations that are worthy of serious study are not only definable in theological terms, but so defining them bridges the gap between research and the findings of practice presented by ministry projects. This integration requires critical theological reflection. In this chapter we will state what we think pastoral/theological reflection is, and elaborate on what we feel are its components, namely: its starting point, its language, its use of reason, its critical and evaluative stance, and its maps and models that guide ministry.

---

[1] Frei, Theology and Narrative, 30.

What Is Theological Reflection?

Christian theological reflection has been defined in a wide variety of ways over many centuries. The resultant pastoral/theological models have been thoroughly articulated by others, for example, Hiltner, Browning, Oden, and Clinebell.[2] For our purposes, we seek a definition that is both pastoral and practical, and which engages ministry in the church and world. Therefore, our view has some compatibility with a tentative definition posted by Stephen Pattison.[3] After many years of teaching pastoral theology, Pattison concludes that a particular entree to theological reflection that students seem to have found helpful is "to suggest that a good starting point for this activity is the model of a critical conversation which takes place between the Christian tradition, the student's own faith presuppositions, and a particular contemporary situation."[4]

With thanks to Pattison, we put our postmodern narrative spin on his definition. Since it is our conviction that the meaning of human life as lived and shared is captured and given communicable structure in story form, we define pastoral theology as:

---

[2] See, Seward Hiltner, *Preface to Pastoral Theology* (New York: Abingdon, 1958); Don S. Browning, *A Fundamental Practical Theology: Descriptive and Strategic Proposals.*(Minneapolis: Fortress Press, 1991); Thomas C. Oden, *Pastoral Theology: Essentials of Ministry* (San Francisco: Harper & Row, 1982); and Howard Clinebell, *Basic Types of Pastoral Care and Counseling* (Nashville: Abingdon, 1984).

[3] James Woodward, Stephen Pattison, and John Patton, *The Blackwell Reader in Pastoral and Practical Theology* (Malden, MA: Blackwell Publishers, 2000).

[4] Stephen Pattison, "Some Straw for the Bricks: A Basic Introduction to Theological Reflection," in *The Blackwell Reader in Pastoral and Practical Theology*, ed. James Woodward, Stephen Pattison, and John Patton (Malden, MA: Blackwell Publishers, 2000), 136.

Critical conversation that takes place at the intersection of
the multiple narratives surrounding a particular
contemporary situation nestled in a particular ministry
context.

This definition allows latitude for discovering what those multiple
narratives are from the context itself, rather than predicting them. It does
seem obvious that the pastoral leader/researcher's personal faith story, the
mediated story of the Christian tradition, including the story of a particular
faith expression (religious institution, denomination, judicatory, sect),
cultural discourse and intergenerational history, and the individual, family,
and group stories surrounding a ministry situation, are among those likely
to intersect around the situation.

Where Do We Begin?

Critical pastoral/theological reflection begins with reflection on
contemporary *situations* confronted in the storied realities of discipleship
and ministry. Such reflection invites the pastoral theologian to raise
questions about what God is doing in the situation, and how the faithful
might join God's transformative action. And, because the situation is
always nestled within a *specific contemporary context*, the wisdom as well
as the folly of that contemporary society and its dominant discourse must
be folded into our reflection. God's intention can, with the Spirit's leading,
be discovered through reflection on the convergence of forces in
contemporary society as well as on, say, the experience of the apostles.
One of the ways God's truth can be discovered is by reading the "human
document."[5]

Explorations of the personal and professional narratives of the
researcher seem to follow after the location of and engagement with the

---

[5] Anton T. Boisen, T*he Exploration of the Inner World: A Study of Mental
Disorder and Religious Experience* (Chicago: Willett, Clark & Company, 1936).

situation in the process of situation analysis. This is because those who study ministry situations tend to both see and interpret through the shady glass of their own experience, thought forms, internalized cultural discourse, and faith group commitments. We have a tendency to miss or ignore the other narratives influencing the situation of ministry. So, there is no such thing as "objective" or "value-free" research in ministry.

Ministry practice and research always launch from the agenda of the religious professional, however covertly it is held. Therefore, we cannot ensure the truth or validity of theological statements arising from our research findings. We can only understand as thoroughly as possible our stories and those that surround a ministry situation, and give voice to what we discern. This allows us to keep them in a more appropriate relationship to the field of study so that they are seen only as one voice in a family of intersecting stories unfolding in the narrative study of the ministry context. It is important to honestly and critically scrutinize what we really hold as religious truth in our own hearts and heads. Using the rigor of critical thinking and reflecting outlined below, it is a worthy effort to search out our own strongly held beliefs and determine how these can be placed in respectful, open engagement with the thought and faith of others.

Next in importance, it seems to us, is our resolve to listen to and reflect upon the multiple, intersecting personal and faith community stories of those who are a part of our ministry settings. These stories reveal how those who serve as church leaders in ministry identify themselves as people of God. Such identifications will clarify the resources of the Christian faith as defined by our traditions that are available for assessing situations involving ethical dilemmas, questions of morality, political power and process, psychological and sociological realities, marriage and family, environmental crises, and pastoral-theological concerns such as suffering, loss, death, evangelism, church structure, discipleship, and future hope.

Finally, theological reflection can be framed by identifying the sources of revelation which lead to insight and theological understanding. In this regard, Albert Outler's widely respected criteria for identifying divine activity in the midst of life are enlightening. Outler's definition of theology in general is instructive as an approach to pastoral theology. He is the author of section 4, Par. 63, of the publication, *Doctrines and Discipline of the United Methodist Church.*[6] This statement, "Our Theological Task," begins with the simple words: "Theology is our effort to reflect upon God's gracious action in our lives." Outler goes on to say that this task is critical and constructive, individual and communal, contextual and incarnational, and essentially practical. He cites four "Sources and Criteria" for guiding our theological task:

> Scripture—the primary source and criterion for Christian doctrine

> Tradition—the story of the church and of God's continuing activity through the history of the church.

> Experience—examination of individual and corporate experience to confirm realities of God's grace attested in scripture.

> Reason—all truth is from God, reason is one way we seek to understand and appropriate that truth.

Outler continues by saying that "[i]n theological reflection, the resources of tradition, experience, and reason are integral to our study of scripture without displacing scripture's primacy for faith and practice."[7]

In this same vein the postmodern narrative researcher asks, "What light do scripture, tradition, experience, and reason throw upon the contemporary situations under study? What do you notice in the analysis of the multiple narratives surrounding a ministry situation that leads you to conclude that these revelatory influences are present? Likewise, how do scripture, tradition, experience, and reason provide windows into understanding the storied experience of the communities to which you minister, and which you will be studying?"

---

[6] United Methodist Church (U.S.), *The Book of Discipline of the United Methodist Church, 2004.* (Nashville: United Methodist Publishing House, 2004),74.

[7] Ibid., 83.

Theological Reflection and Reason

In our judgment, the capacity to think and reason is a gift from God to be put into divine service, as is any other gift to the faithful. God is the basis of all reason (in the order of being, see John 1) but reason is a basis of knowledge of God (in the order of knowing). Even our intuitive knowing is often tested and assessed as sound or unsound on the basis of logical reflection.[8]

Traditionally, theologians seem to have put two basic forms of reasoning into service in theological reflection: deductive and inductive forms of reasoning. *Deductive reasoning* starts with the general and moves to the particular, in a cause-and-effect manner. It begins *a priori*, prior to looking at the specific facts. *Inductive reasoning* starts with the particular and moves to the general, in an effect-to cause manner, as is the case with modern western scientific investigation. Each of these logical forms of thinking can give structure to theological methods or whole paradigms.

Deductive Reasoning

Thomas Oden is a professor emeritus of systematic theology at Drew whose pastoral and theological work takes deductive logic as its starting point. Oden believes that deducing the wisdom of the centuries from the works of our pre-modern theological forbears in the church will overcome what he deems the errors and erosions of contemporary Christian faith practices. Such a recovery yields a pastoral theology that deals with the office and function of the pastor.

> Pastoral theology is that branch of Christian theology that deals with the office and functions of the pastor. It is theology because it treats of the consequences of God's self-disclosure in history. It is pastoral because it deals

---

[8] Norman L. Geisler and Ronald M. Brooks, *Come, Let Us Reason: An Introduction to Logical Thinking* (Grand Rapids, MI: Baker Book House, 1990).

with those consequences as they pertain to the roles, task, duties, and work of the pastor.[9]

Edward Thurneysen launches his pastoral theology from the foundational notion that all pastoral care is a disciplined conversation between pastoral caregivers and persons they serve that communicates the Word of God. The aim of such conversation is to lead the person back to sermon and sacraments in the worship of the church. Influenced by Barth, Harnack, and others, Thurneysen's work represents a deductive approach to pastoral theology wherein biblically based doctrine is brought into the consciousness of the counselee to facilitate transformation and healing.[10]

Inductive Reasoning

Seward Hiltner, a pioneer in the field of pastoral theology who taught at Princeton University, employs inductive reasoning as his starting place. Hiltner defines pastoral theology as "that branch or field of theological knowledge and inquiry that brings the shepherding perspective to bear upon all the operations and functions of the church and the minister, and then draws conclusions of a theological order from reflection on these observations."[11] Hiltner sees pastoral diagnosis of situations of concern as "[g]rasping the essence of a matter so as to know what to do." Extending his view of creation as the unity of all things, his hermeneutical principle is to study what Boisen called "living human documents" (identified earlier) and not just human psychology, but human beings in all of their wholeness

---

[9] Thomas C. Oden, *Pastoral Theology: Essentials of Ministry* (San Francisco: Harper & Row, 1982), x.

[10] See Eduard Thurneysen, *A Theology of Pastoral Care* (Richmond, Va.: John Knox Press, 1962).

[11] Seward Hiltner, "The Meaning and Importance of Pastoral Theology," in *The Blackwell Reader in Pastoral and Practical Theology*, edited by James Woodward, Stephen Pattison, and John Patton (Malden, MA: Blackwell Publishers, 2000), 28.

and complexity.[12] Hiltner adapts Tillich's method of correlation for this purpose, raising questions and answers about contemporary culture as well as faith traditions, and finding their theologically meaningful relationship by attending to the correspondence of their descriptive metaphors.[13]

Charles Gerkin employs inductive and deductive reasoning as he explicates the understanding gained when Christians in faith communities explore the intersection of the meaning of their distinctive faith stories and the meanings they experience in their situational stories of contemporary experience in the world.[14]

Abductive Reasoning

In the postmodern era, yet another starting point for the appropriation of theological knowledge has come to the fore. Leonard Sweet, Brian McClaren, and Jerry Haselmayer describe in their recent book, *"A" Is for Abduction: The Language of the Emerging Church*, what they call the "abductive method" for seeking theological knowledge. Drawing upon the writings of K.T. Fann's interpretation of Charles Pierce's theory of abductions (Sweet, et. al.) advocate a method of theological communication in which the discourse of the communicator "seizes" the *imagination* of people and transports them from their current thought and imagined world to another, with transformative results. The authors note that Jesus used parables to "kidnap" the consciousness of his hearers, taking his listeners by surprise so that their perspective on the world was radically changed.

---

[12] See Seward Hiltner, *Preface to Pastoral Theology* (New York: Abingdon, 1958), 51.

[13] Hiltner's Lecture Notes, Princeton Theological Seminary, 1966.

[14] Charles V. Gerkin, *Widening the Horizons: Pastoral Responses to a Fragmented Society* (Philadelphia: Westminster Press, 1986), 61.

A contemporary version of the abductive method can be found in the Lake Wobegon tales of Garrison Keillor, they say. [15]

Abduction is a mode of fiction rather than logic. It is neither deductive nor inductive. It is nonlogical. It is sensory. The intellect's intuitive quest for a "true" picture of the world is served a sensory banquet in the form of stories that relate human experience.

While research in ministry may employ theological language that includes any or all of these forms of reasoning, it seems to us that the abductive form is more consonant with narrative analysis and theological description of ministry situations. It is also more likely than other models and methods to help us unpack the metaphors and meanings embedded in the storied experience of religious communities.

Critical Thinking and Theological Reflection

Critical thinking puts in service the forms of reflection described above. It also has been touted as the scholar's protection against biased research. We do not hold that an absolute protection from bias is possible, but we do value critical thinking for other sound reasons. Critical thinking does keep the scholar's eyes and ears open, the sweep of perception wider, and appreciation of the depths of knowledge visible to the researcher. Also, it refuses to universalize its perceptions. It encourages a search for truth that is patient, appreciative of diverse, even conflicting, ideas, and is always open to new experiences, ideas, and knowledge. It also promotes modesty in claims for one's own ideas and willingness to subject these to the critical evaluation of others. In doctoral programs students are expected to hold to high standards of critical reflection, even as they honestly articulate their own convictions.

---

[15] Leonard I. Sweet, Brian D. McLaren, and Jerry Haselmayer, *"A" Is for Abductive: The Language of the Emerging Church* (Grand Rapids, MI: Zondervan, 2003), 31–33. 56

Critical thinking expressed in verbal or written forms of discourse is a process that embraces the following responses:

Reading or listening to the descriptive data (stories; found documents; research such as books, lectures, films; lectures; observations; ideas; events; etc.) with openness and curiosity. A great many scholarly mistakes, distortions, misinterpretations and failures occur because scholars do not put in the effort to really understand what has been said before proceeding to reflect or criticize. Studying ideas, descriptive stories, and organized research information enough to understand what their makers are saying helps us avoid shallow scholarship!

Thinking about the contexts out of which presenters (lecturers, authors) or storytellers speak. From which ethnic, gendered, cultural, religious, academic, personal, and social contexts do the presenters emerge? What do you know about the presenters that might shape their thought? How does the language they use (discourse) disclose their identity, values, intellectual and spiritual commitments, and location in the social fabric?

Thinking about the contexts out of which we spring. Which of the religious, ethnic, gendered, cultural, academic, personal, or social contexts of your own life and development may be influencing how you are hearing or interpreting ideas you have come upon?

Distinguishing for ourselves between important and relevant data, and data or information that is not as relevant or important. It's easy to get sidetracked and miss the essentials of what is presented.

Comparing and contrasting the ideas or stories presented with our own ideas or stories. Good scholarship draws from as many sources as possible for comparisons. What similarities and differences do you discern in the thought or discourse of the various authors, presenters, or storytellers you are consulting?

Forming tentative hypotheses about the influences that impact the concern or opportunity and possible solutions you are seeking. Test these hypotheses through engagement and consultation with those who have lived with the concern or opportunity as well as with others who have worked on it, or who may have a fresh perspective.

Drawing your own tentative conclusions, based upon what you have learned so far. Try them out in your discourse with others. Remain non-defensive and open to learning as others respond to your ideas and conclusions with affirmation or challenge. There is no shame in changing an intellectual position or commitment when this change is informed by new learning or experience.

Continuing to learn from critical thinking about these ideas or concern/opportunities. Check a wide variety of sources, including talking to people face-to-face to tease out ideas, test preferred or alternative stories, and find practical solutions.

Theology and Social/Scientific Method

When we undertake to make a theological appraisal of a situation, we may wish to draw upon the tools of secular research, particularly those of social science, since these tools have allowed generations of researchers to reach more deeply into the mysteries of human consciousness, development, personality, behavior, and thought process,. But we should not do so uncritically. Any method we employ is likely to be grounded in some social/scientific tradition and its under-girding philosophy or slant on reality. This must be considered an engaging and useful narrative, not a defining metaphor for all reality.

Theological Thinking and Pastoral Theology

So that theologians can talk sensibly, at least to each other, they have a mutual understanding of the ways they use language to describe their research findings and talk about God, the church, ministry, and theological "truth." Part of what they commonly assume is that there are three "orders" of scholarly language by means of which they frame their ideas and allow them to communicate with others.[16]

First Order Language

First order theological language is explicit God language. God language appears in the stories, liturgies, hymns, prayers, and gestures of a faith tradition that describe the way in which persons or communities of faith are related to God. For Christians, of course, the Bible is the primary source of first order theological language. For theologians, God language may take the form of abstractions, metaphors, images, and stories. The narrative theologian looks with respect upon all of these as useful, descriptive particularities of an indescribable mystery.

Second Order Language

Second order language is language that theologians use in the explication and critical evaluation or appropriation of the basic meaning of the stories, liturgies, hymns, prayers, and gestures of a faith tradition. Second order reflection yields theological judgments or proposals, which eventually can be accepted as doctrine by a faith community, such as the doctrine of papal infallibility or of predestination.

Third Order Language

Third order language is language theologians use when critically evaluating the sources, norms, and procedures used by those who make theological judgments and arrive at claims of religious truth. This includes pastoral theology and theological method.

Theology is our effort to make God accessible to our understanding. This may also help ourselves and others find our way to God. Theology is made with human hands. It is partial, incomplete, and limited, while God

---

[16] See T. W. Jennings, Jr., "Pastoral Theological Methodology," in *Dictionary of Pastoral Care and Counseling*, ed. Rodney J. Hunter (Nashville: Abingdon, 1990), 862.

remains a full, expansive, holy mystery. But the traveler needs a map, however poor it may be, to find his or her way. Michael Christensen's map for theological reflection on spiritual pilgrimage and ministry involves the theologian's mystical apprehension of divine revelation, discerned through intuition centered on the heart, faithfully applied in following the vision of three streams from the divine Source—Father, Son, and Holy Spirit—realized in Worship, Community, and Mission.[17]

Another map, one created for theological reflection on modern evangelism, comes from the work of Professor Leonard Sweet. In his model, or map, he employs the discernment and appropriation of contemporary images as his hermeneutical principle, citing their capacity to evoke spiritual response, transformation and change. He then attempts to connect these meaningfully with the Christian tradition.[18]

Students who intend to utilize any of these maps, or other pastoral theologies, in their projects will need to study them more thoroughly and carefully. We will offer some tools which can certainly help you as you form your ministry projects and define and use your theological stance in reflecting upon your ministry situations. My grandfather (Bill's) used to tell me to choose the "the right tool for the right job." Approaches to theological reflection are tools, selected because they seem to provide the "right" guidance to pastoral practice for a particular ministry situation. Sometimes the situation calls for a simple, generally drawn map. At other times, especially in dealing with complex and difficult issues such as religious and cultural warfare, world hunger, bioengineering, in-vitro conception, cloning, artificially intelligent computers, euthanasia, the uses of nuclear power, etc., more detailed maps for theological reflection are needed.

---

[17] Michael J. Christensen and Carl E. Savage, *Equipping the Saints: Mobilizing Laity for Ministry* (Nashville: Abingdon, 2000), 161.

[18] Lecture, Drew University, Madison, NJ, Summer 2000, and numerous books.

Our theological maps can quickly become outdated in these times. We need to keep developing new ones with which to greet the "earthquakes" of change and development of human society. In fact, criticisms of modern and postmodern theologies are legitimate and are frequently expressed in the scholarly world. Our take on these theological maps is that they tend to focus too narrowly on the office and function of the pastor or professional theologian. They can foster clericalism, and bias towards the higher spiritual status of clergy in comparison to the laity. Thus, the priesthood of all believers, which holds equal positions for all believers in the theological discourse of the church, is limited.

Another criticism that can be lodged with makers of modern and postmodern theologies is that the context for theological reflection has not been taken seriously enough. Theologians and practitioners have tended to interpose thought forms, language, and preconceived cultural perceptions in their observations and reflections on ministerial context. While the latter is inevitable, pastoral theological models should account for this bias and provide a disciplined framework for accounting for contextual concerns.

It is also our lament that the validity of theological wisdom gained through the experience of persons from various faith communities has not been duly regarded. Further, the prophetic ingredient in theological reflection has been neglected, and issues of social and interpersonal justice have been ignored, downplayed, or seen as outside the realm of pastoral care. And, further, practical moral guidance and spiritual discipline have not been thoroughly reflected upon or communicated intentionally or effectively enough.

Finally, pastoral theologians have not been careful enough to explain their hermeneutical principles, i.e., principles employed in the interpretations they make of scripture, of the historical narrative of the church's tradition, or of personal, corporate, and cultural experience. For instance, the human sciences, including social science, approach their declarations of scientific truth as though they were value-neutral, universally applicable, and distant from the particular, value-laden influences on their thought that are inherent in their methodologies. Critiquing these methods is becoming increasingly important, as Don S. Browning observes:

Theologians and churches have increasingly both used and
envied the human sciences. This is reflected in a number of
phenomena: (1) The psychological disciplines have
influenced the counseling and pastoral care disciplines of
the church enormously. (2) Sociology influences liberation
and political theologies, church planners, and the thinking
of all educated church people. (3) Anthropology, and
especially through anthropological study of ritual and
initiation processes, influence liturgics and religious
education. (4) The psychology of moral development
(Kohlberg, Gilligan) and developmental psychology
(Freud, Erickson) have had tremendous impact on our
understandings of both human and Christian maturity.[19]

Partly as a correction to the above, some contemporary pastoral
theologians have offered models for pastoral/theological reflection that
deserve attention.

Don S. Browning, cited above, develops what he calls a fundamental
Practical Theology, wherein critical/theological reflection moves from
practice to theory and back to practice. His is a modified method of
correlation that borrows from Tillich and Tracy. It provides an interpretive
principle, or hermeneutic, similar to the understanding of practical reason
of Aristotle (*phronesis*).[20] Since all epistemological approaches are value-
laden, the most truthful way to go about describing and trying to
understand a given branch of human knowledge, including theology, is to
describe and analyze its meta-narrative, the story of its tradition.[21]

---

[19] Don S. Browning, *A Fundamental Practical Theology: Descriptive and
Strategic Proposals* (Minneapolis: Fortress Press, 1991), 80–81.

[20] Browning, *A Fundamental Practical Theology*, 11

[21] Browning, *A Fundamental Practical Theology*, 11

Citing Jürgen Habermas as his authority, Browning argues that "all communication entails claims about the comprehensibility, truth, truthfulness, and rightness of what is said."[22] All theology should be subsumed under a fundamental practical theology, including systematic, historical, and descriptive theologies, all subject to critical analysis not only of their claims, but of the very values underlying the methods by which they arrive at those claims.[23] For Browning, fundamental practical theology is a "critical correlational practical theology which must support its implicit validity claims if it takes part in the discourse of a free society aimed at shaping the common good."[24] It proceeds by addressing concrete situations, and "[c]ritically correlates both questions and answers found in Christian faith with questions and implied answers in various secular perspectives (the human sciences, the arts), on common human experience."[25] Browning insists that in approaching any situation of ministry, whether within a religious or secular context, moral/theological conclusions about what is going on and what to do about it be subject to five validity claims, all of which are common to practical thinking:

> (1) the visional level (which inevitably raises metaphysical validity claims); (2) the obligational level (which raises normative ethical claims, or claims of rightness in Habermas's sense of this word); (3) the tendency-need or anthropological dimension (which raises claims about human nature, its basic human needs, and the kinds of pre-moral goods required to meet those needs—a discussion that Habermas believes is impossible

---

[22] Browning, *A Fundamental Practical Theology*, 69.

[23] Browning, *A Fundamental Practical Theology*, 7-8.

[24] Browning, *A Fundamental Practical Theology*, 71

[25] Don Browning, "Pastoral Theology in a Pluralistic Age," in *The Blackwell Reader in Pastoral and Practical Theology*, ed. James Woodward, Stephen Pattison, and John Patton (Malden, MA: Blackwell Publishers, 2000), 93.

to conduct); (4) an environmental-social dimension (which raises claims that deal primarily with social-systemic and ecological constraints on our tendencies and needs); and (5) the rule-role dimension (which raises claims about the concrete patterns we should enact in our actual praxis in the everyday world).[26]

Such a procedure, he says, advances the possibility that the pastoral care intervention will have credibility and acceptance in the real world.

A second postmodern attempt to frame a model for pastoral and practical theology is put forward by Pattison, introduced above. Pattison sees descriptive theology, most often used in analysis of pastoral situations, care and counseling, as reflection on the discourse (story, narrative) surrounding the engagement of tradition, personal faith, and situation. Discernment of theological insight (revelation of what God is doing) surfaces in the process, and conclusions provide a working truth, which evolves through further reflection, to put to use in ministry. For Pattison, theological reflection embraces "a model of a critical conversation which takes place between the Christian tradition, the student's own faith presuppositions and a particular contemporary situation." Pattison continues to say that the model is simple, not original, and borrows from other models. But if it is explored, it will become more complex.[27]

These are some of the maps drawn by premodern and modern pastoral theologians to aid us in our search for the truth of God in the midst of life, practical wisdom that informs what we do in theological reflection and its application in ministry. While continuing to think in modern scientific terms, Browning and Pattison move pastoral-theological discussion in the direction of looking at diversity, and multiplicity of influences on Christian community dynamics, and the need for the observer to examine her/his own perceptual apparatus.

---

[26] Browning, *A Fundamental Practical Theology*, 71

[27] Pattison, "Theological Reflection," 136. 72

A Postmodern Approach to Research
and Pastoral Theology in Ministry

How can postmodern congregational realities be more adequately grasped by narrative methodology? The human thirst for God, and the hope, guidance, healing, and transformation God brings to human life is great. But where do we find God? How do we discern God's presence with assurance? When we attempt to answer these questions we cannot help but tell a story. Theology is the story that epresses our experience with God. By means of it we explain and maintain our connection with the divine.

When people are called to faith their life is formed around meaning systems into which have been poured socially-constructed ways of being, behaving, and spiritually observing. But the researcher of faith communities must always look among these social constructions and see the intangible, the shadow story, the preferred, God-engendered meanings derived from the Biblical narratives, communicated across generations, and refreshed by current God experience.

Theological discernment attempts to determine the "realness and rightness" of these meanings by examining situations of ministry in which they are either latent or are breaking through. This aspect of the narrative uncovered in research is intuitively grasped and distinctive from the sometimes toxic social constructions among which it may be nested and from which it must be teased apart. The object of this form of research and theological reflection is to provide understanding and useful guidance to the faith community and the unfolding ministries it attempts.

It is our view that all postmodern theology is descriptive theology. Pastoral theology is the product of abductive hovering over the faith-storied experiences human beings find meaningful, and discerning and describing these meanings so that they make sense. The way in which faith communities realize and share what they hold dear and meaningful to them is through the generation of stories. These stories capture their ever-changing faith experience and embody the words, symbols, rituals and other actions that have formed them and will form new generations of believers. When sampled at a moment in time they are like snapshots of a faith community's compiled identity, historical expressions, faithful praxis,

and imagined futures. The researcher can only claim what she/he sees at
the moment of observation, the "what is" of the now. Sampling the next
moments, weeks, months, and years will likely generate a different finding
and description. Simply stated, the vehicle that delivers theological
guidance to the church and its ministries is language, and that language
tells a story. Various branches of theology along with the philosophical and
social science constructs and methods that interact with them are scripts, or
narrative plans, that intersect with the wider story of faith. They are a part
of its composition; or they embellish, or "thicken" the faith story. The
researcher assesses their contribution to the meanings uncovered in
storytelling by using the tools of social analysis. The researcher is
especially interested in how the assumed notions of the realities of life and
faith are embedded in social discourse and internalized by the faith
community, for these may be blocking a preferred, alternative story that
could be transformative for the community.

When applied to the study of faith communities, this postmodern,
narrative approach is guided by the following observations:

First, these communities live, move, and have their being through the
formative experiences their members have with the divine. From
interacting with the biblical narratives and the prayers, hymns, and
worship events which characterize the faith story and make God real to
them, members draw meanings out of which their identity is constructed.
They are formed in faith, spoken into being. Their story and God's story
have increasing congruency. They draw both spiritual orientation and
ethical guidance from their encounter with God as seen in Jesus Christ and
experienced continuously in the Spirit. The Spirit "interlaces" the human
story with the biblical narratives, resulting in transforming consequences.
Discipleship in faith communities is empowered by a sense of the
rightness and authenticity (plain sense) of religious truths that come to
them as their eyes are opened to the divine in acts of devotion and service.
These tentatively held truths guide them. This "plain sense" of the
presence of God in community amounts to arrival at an operational
understanding of what divine action is effecting in a specific ministry
context. It is attained through careful reflection upon intersecting, told
stories surrounding an important concern or opportunity that has surfaced

in the consciousness of the community. It is grasped intuitively, captured in the observer's sensory awareness and imagination as a confluence of practical reason, uncovered meanings, perceptions of difference, and evidence of ministry fruits nurtured by divine love, justice, and care of creation. It is a working theological truth. Nevertheless, the community's personal and corporate life is organized and at times transformed by this communal discernment and made manifest in ministry. Community relationship dynamics and order are based on faithfully grasped evidence of their rightness, or fit, with the biblical narratives of the life and work of Jesus and His forbears in the tradition, especially from biblical teachings of love, justice, and care of creation made manifest in the actions and relationships of the faith community.

Second, the valuing of gifts, variation of contextual circumstances, mutuality, and consensual practice is consistent in community life. Acts of devotion and service are organized around these meanings and are continuous. In these ways the authentic community's story is borne forward by language, a distinctive discourse, and by symbols that transmit and give continuity to the community's religious meaning system over time. These theological meanings are ever-changing, not static, and continue to emerge as long as interaction with the divine is maintained.

A Multi-Sensory Narrative Hermeneutic

Hermeneutics has to do with the principles of interpretation and explanation by which theologians are guided as they hover over the storied meanings they observe in the study of faith communities. The discernment of the presence of God in faith communities is always to be undertaken with humility and with a stance of curiosity and suspended judgment. By careful interviewing, study, and dialogue with participants in the faith community, the researcher seeks to "hear" the whole story of the people of God, grasp the new thing God may be doing in the life of the community, and reflect upon its implications for the future. More evident at first in the unfolding narratives are the internalized, culturally conditioned parts of the whole, which contain the images and discourse of the dominant culture in which the faith community resides as well as negative memories or traumatic events that have damaged its identity and stressed or limited its ministries. But buried there also are the unspoken meanings, faith aspirations, and human hopes that have been beaten down and subjugated to the more powerful messages of the culture. With attentiveness to the language in which the community's experience is embedded, researchers utilize story analysis to externalize these preferred, "shadow" scripts, connect their meanings, assess their importance to ministry, give them an audience, and encourage their development. When these unearthed meanings are validated in the understanding and faith of the community, they represent an opening for God's transforming power to take hold. In theological reflection based on engagement with the story, resourced by emerging meanings teased apart from the dominant story, the pastoral theologian facilitates the imagination of new futures of faith and action within the community. Old rigidities and stagnation can yield to a new and dynamic order in the community, based not on hierarchical notions of power and status, but on gifts, variety of circumstances, fellowship, and consensual practice of ministry.

Further, study of a narrative of concern or opportunity in faith communities is, in some sense, like taking a snapshot. All that the researcher can say is that, at this time and in this context, these are the meanings that have been observed by the researcher and participant team, shared in the community and identified as authentic by the prayerful reflection of the community. The researcher, with the team, obtains this snapshot by means of listening to the multiple, intertwining narratives that cluster about a particular ministry concern or opportunity. However, "listening" as we will be using it here is more than audition or hearing with ears. The ministry researcher does not only listen with ears, but opens up all her/his personal sensory apparatus and puts it at the disposal of theological awareness.

How does this work in practice? Some examples of how a researcher of faith communities may gain a sense of the realness and rightness of a whole story surrounding a concern or opportunity are these:

❖ Hearing the rumble and feeling the vibration of an elevated train passing by a struggling inner city church so as to enter into the rhythms of urban life that shape the experience of worshippers;

❖ Interrupting a conversation with a citizen who is describing the quality of life in his community to ask about the sewer smells emanating from faulty septic systems saturating the town, still used because of political resistance to connecting to a new sewer trunk line;

❖ Hearing the slightly angry tone of voice a parishioner uses when characterizing a former pastor, or the jubilation of a youth who has finally found a spiritual home in the church; connecting these stories to the concern about the church's

❖ leadership history, or to the opportunity for ministry that opened up when the reluctant church provided space and leadership for a youth program;

❖ Tasting the quality of food that has been lovingly prepared for fundraising dinners by the same faithful hands for the past forty years;

❖ Touching the rough texture of a church pew and pondering its effect on the spirituality of the worshippers;

❖ Intuiting the meaning behind the carefully protective wording of the minutes of a church board's discussions about becoming an open and affirming congregation;

❖ Listening to and reflecting on a number of conflicting stories describing a traumatic incident that forever changed a community and submerged it in shame and regret; detecting the faint outline of an alternative, preferred but captive story waiting to be told.

So, in this approach, the researcher opens her/his senses as though they were windows to the story, each allowing light into the consciousness of the observer/researcher in the form of unique views, a cacophony of sounds, the subtle blend of alternative odors, a variety of textures, and, of course, a plethora of reports on storied experience. Like anthropologists, researchers of faith communities fuel their reflection with impressions from the research site provided by their senses. However, the perceptions gained are guided and sharpened by a consciousness formed by immersion in the usual practices of a faith community. Interaction with the divine in worship through engagement with word and sacraments hone these perceptions and form within the faithful the internal meanings and inclinations towards interpretive insight that equip them to reflect on the stories of the community. Trusting that the true story that emerges is authentic because it is transparent, not hidden, and thus suffused with the divine Spirit, the researcher works with the community team to coauthor the new story.

CHAPTER 3

Learning from the Story of The Faith Community

Biblical story, literary story, biographical story, church story. These and many other narratives interlace to reveal who Jesus Christ is for us today. Knowing that, or at least something of who Jesus is for us today, we can then know who we are for one another, for the creation itself, and within God's intentions.[1]

***

The study of a ministry site is a ministry in and of itself. That is, to arrive at a sense of the current self-understanding of a religious community often has the attendant benefits of aiding in theological discernment within that body and also of providing direction for the generation of relevant and effective ministries.

In chapter one, we briefly contrasted modern with postmodern approaches to ministry research and outlined a distinctive narrative methodology for a postmodern approach. In chapter two we provided the reader with a picture of the theological dimension of this approach and

---

[1] Barnes, *The Story of Discipleship*, 51.

described our narrative hermeneutic. In this chapter, we present the postmodern approach in action, walking the researcher through the process of gaining awareness of the work of God in a given community by learning from its story. The important meanings by which communities of faith live are revealed in the stories they tell about their experience as communities of faith, even when the discourse is narrowed to the ministry concern or opportunity to be researched.

In what follows, we will describe to the reader some of the process of narrative analysis of ministry concerns and opportunities. Then, we will present the "Postmodern Narrative Approach to Ministry Research" in summary form and demonstrate its use in an actual ministry situation.

The Process of Narrative Analysis

Evoking Stories from the Situation

We become skilled at evoking stories from the ministry situation by first claiming and understanding our own stories as leaders/researchers. Those who lead and would study their faith communities inevitably participate in the very myopia they seek to remedy through research. Therefore, essential to the elucidation of the whole story of a concern or opportunity faced by a faith community is attaining a grasp of the ways in which *the researcher's own story* intersects with the narrative of concern or opportunity and the multiple narratives that engage with it. Our own stories and the meanings with which they are suffused—meanings that we hold dear—are to some extent projected onto our research efforts and shape our presence as students and facilitators of change in these communities.

Now, we cannot discard our own histories, nor should we try. Rather, in this approach, researchers, as well as those who participate with them, are more likely to evoke a true story of the faith community if they first study and claim the storied influences of their own birth families, cultural contexts, education, social experience, theological outlook, faith tradition, and preferred ways to do and participate in ministry. For these influences together are the lens through which they see and describe what they study. Hence, those who do research in ministry themselves may need to recognize how their identities have been shaped by their dominant cultural messages. These cultural messages are organized in the form of internalized story lines, or scripts, that shape their perceptions of reality, choices and behavior. There are many kinds of scripts people carry around within, but each person has made choices about which internal voice(s) to follow. This is usually the script that reflects the dominant culture in which the person is located, but it may not tell a full story, or even a preferred one, which may lurk behind it, hidden and unexpressed (shadow script). For instance, a person may have grown up in a culture where men are seen, and expected to behave as, the "strong ones."

Yet they may yearn for a relational style that is egalitarian, relational, and free of gender bias.[2] *Externalizing* and giving voice to this alternative, shadow story can bring change and healing.

Leaders/researchers are dramatically influenced by their dominant scripts, past or current shadow scripts, and other internalized, organized story lines, just as are those whom they study in personal or community ministry sites. Their scripts largely determine the ways in which they read and interpret the storied data they gather. Hence, the leader's/researcher's self-awareness extends to establishing the *role of the leader/researcher in this postmodern approach*. The elements of this role are numerous.

First, the leader/researcher is a *story broker*. By drawing out the multiple narratives that intersect around a concern or opportunity, the researcher facilitates a faith community's negotiation between a *problem-saturated story* (an existing negative state or condition that concerns them or a potential not yet realized) and a *preferred, emerging story* (a new state or condition that excites them and advances God's ministry among them).

---

[2] Joan D. Atwood, "Social Construction Theory and Therapy Assumptions," in *Family Scripts*, edited by Joan D. Atwood (Washington, DC: Accelerated Development, 1996), 12–22.

Stating it metaphorically, the leader/researcher encourages people to "sing out" their new song, and sings along with them.

Second, the postmodern leader/researcher assumes a *kenotic position* as a handler of people's stories. That is, to the extent possible, the researcher empties her/himself of preconceptions, paradigms of interpretation, or presumptions about the stories that emerge. In addition, the researcher looks within the tangled and sometimes confusing maze of intermeshing narratives for clues that may guide interpretation of a narrative of concern or opportunity. Specifically, the researcher keeps an especially sharp eye out for moments when a community or persons reveal their emerging, preferred story and break into their new song, however fleeting these moments might be.

Third, the leader/researcher remains as self-differentiated and non-reactive as possible. When people share their stories they frequently come into conflict with those whose outlook on a concern or opportunity is quite different than their own. People perceive difference from others in their personal and social lives because their defining narratives, or stories, are unique, as are their individual and corporate contexts. Therefore, their ways of discerning meaning and organizing their lives are distinctive, frequently leading to a perception of difference. Postmodern ministry research therefore affirms that addressing differences adds to learning and growth. Difference is not only tolerable, it is to be embraced, processed with patience and understanding, orchestrated by the leader into new configurations of community collaboration and ministry, and celebrated. Persons who participate in this research may become anxious in relating their own stories or in listening to the stories of others. The researcher's calm demeanor and assurances that differences are expected and conflict a normal and useful part of arriving at a true story, add to a safe storytelling environment.

Joining with the Research Team and Faith Community

"Joining," which describes relationship interactions in human groups, is a term widely used in family therapy literature. It refers to the reality that leaders (such as therapists or clergy leaders) are seldom able to influence those they would lead without first becoming meaningful participants in their common life. Leaders/researchers do not necessarily have to be inducted as "one of" the community they would study any more than an anthropologist does in the study of a culture. But leaders/researchers must relate with humanity, compassion, understanding, respect, and sensitivity so as to be trusted by those who tell their stories. Part of this amounts to the ability to put people at ease, value the diversity of personal styles and language forms people use when they share of themselves, maintain appropriate personal boundaries, and keep confidences when asked to do so. Such joining takes time and patience. However, many leaders of faith communities have already established both credibility and trust among their constituent members. This usually extends to new projects the leader introduces, such as Doctor of Ministry research initiatives. Yet, the leader should determine beforehand whether enough rapport with the faith group has been established, and whether adequate support for the research project is likely to be given.

A successful Doctor of Ministry research project is not a solo undertaking. In fact, working with a select laity team who will help identify the focus of research, help plan, execute, and evaluate it, and remain in reflective theological dialogue with the leader/researcher, is a requirement of the postmodern narrative approach. The team should be persons of maturity, faith, and sound judgment. To the extent feasible, the team membership should be diverse in gifts, socio-economic status, and cultural and ethnic makeup. It should seek to model openness to the Spirit through the synergistic interaction of team member gifts, and it should consist of persons with whom the leader/researcher can work effectively, productively, and joyfully. Such laity teams most often find the project team experience exhilarating and rewarding. They report having experienced genuine lay-clergy collaboration and the priesthood of all believers in a refreshing new way. When given this chance, they are often ready to go to work and are quite devoted and open to the new experience.

Defining a Narrative of Concern
or Opportunity

In our judgment, research in ministry is the most productive when it is
carefully and modestly designed. A promising beginning for such research
is identifying the point of intersection of the multiple narratives that
surface around a story, or narrative of concern, or opportunity that has
arisen in the community's awareness or experience. Each of these
intersecting narratives is likely to provide a particular slant on the concern
or opportunity. Listening to and reflecting on each of these stories brings
the researcher closer to an informed awareness and working understanding
of the concern or opportunity. Each of the narratives "thickens" in depth
and insight the description of the concern or opportunity and of any
preferred, emerging, alternative story that will become the impetus and
guide for future action. And, because the identity of a congregation or
other ministry site is shaped by its ever-changing story, clarity about its
current identity may also surface through this research. Decades ago
Gregory Bateson, anthropologist and psychologist, made the social science
community more aware of the subjective nature of reality and of learning.[3]
As shown in his discussion of "news of difference," which refers to the
tension between what is said and what is not said, Bateson was convinced
that new learning occurs when human beings are presented with a
comparison of one set of events in time with another. Building upon this,
family theorist Michael White observed that many families with whom he
worked adapted to their problems and were not aware of the ways in which
these problems affected the rest of their lives because they could not see
the difference between what was and what could be.[4] Human beings seem

---

[3] See Gregory. Bateson, *Mind and Nature a Necessary Unity*, Advances in
Systems Theory, Complexity, and the Human Sciences (Cresskill, N.J.: Hampton
Press, 2002) or Gregory. Bateson, Steps to an Ecology of Mind (Chicago:
University of Chicago Press, 2000).

[4] Gerald Monk, "How Narrative Therapy Works," in *Narrative Therapy in
Practice: the Archaeology of Hope* (San Francisco: Jossey-Bass Publishers, 1997),
7

to sail along under the power of one set of guiding thoughts and are not likely to change until they are presented with credible and promising alternatives.

What is true of families is patently true of many faith communities and those who lead them. Congregations and other religious bodies are often strangely unaware of how their defining, dominant discourses serve to obscure a latent, more functional, faithful, and hopeful story. They simply do not "get it" that within the hearts of the people there are other meaningful, more exciting, and promising yearnings for and knowledge of faith practice that represent the captive potentials of God's new story for them. Atwood, the postmodern scholar of narrative theory cited previously,[5] reminds us that shadow scripts are those alternative internal (though not unconscious) plans that do not square with the dominant script, and are opposite from it. They contain the things not said, behaviors not attempted, and gestures that have not been made.

It follows that, if revealed and acted upon, shadow scripts represent the seeds of change and of more authentic living. Or, if these are negative self or other perceptions that are externalized and irresponsibly claimed and acted upon, they can be self-destructive and lead to broken relationships. On the other hand, the sharing of problematic shadow scripts responsibly in a secure and caring fellowship can lead to redemption and a more authentic and integrated faith. For instance, church members who confront their own secret yearnings to be professional church leaders (shadow script), and own the disruptive and competitive behaviors that express this conflict, can be freed to serve God with their own unique gifts (preferred story). Or, a faith community, whose public face is open and inclusive (dominant discourse), comes to grips with a long-standing, covert practice of ignoring and marginalizing "certain types" of people (shadow script) and re-stories itself to face its demons and be intentionally inclusive. Such realizations can be painful, but can also lead to change and renewal.

---

[5] Atwood, "Social Construction Theory and Therapy Assumptions," 16.

Faith communities have both kinds of shadow scripts described above. When they are shared and embraced in faith, they may either lead to the resolution of inner conflicts or to the emergence of a preferred, more hopeful story. Nevertheless, faith communities often remain under the influence of dominant story scripts that define them and that are maintained by the personally and culturally prescribed language and practices of the community at work and worship. These communities are heavily influenced in structure and character by their specific socio-cultural, geographical, ethnic *contexts*. Sometimes they simply plunge ahead, with little sensitivity to the ways they disallow a diversity of voices to be heard, or how they thwart their own hidden, exciting potentials for creating ministries of challenge and care. Less dominant, or marginalized, members frequently remain mute, preventing the orchestration of newer and fuller divine music. Thus, they miss out on the alternative stories waiting to be told and made manifest in ministry.

Grasping the features of narrative process at work in faith communities is good preparation for the *formative stage* of the Doctor of Ministry project. Even so, leaders/researchers sometimes struggle to define their ministry projects sufficiently. Arranging a period of careful listening to the process at work at a ministry site and consulting with the leaders of the faith community may help one decide upon the type of project they will undertake. Acceptable types include projects that enhance the life of a congregation or community setting, i.e., projects that deal with ministries of mercy and justice.

During this stage, the goal is to arrive at a clear outline description of a specific concern or opportunity in the practice of ministry that is researchable and manageable within a certain time frame. Leaders/researchers should be attentive to the specific context in which the ministry situation is nestled, name the theological/theoretical stance they will be taking, begin to think of which research methods to use, and estimate the work required and the time necessary to complete it.

Leaders/researchers who are assuming this role for the first time may find themselves vulnerable to some of the common problems that arise in the formative stage. These include such things as: failure to recruit, train, and work with a Lay Advisory Committee; indecision about selecting a ministry project; and, isolation (failure to stay connected to colleagues and faculty). *Online students* should be especially alert to the latter.

Evoking, Listening to, and Deconstructing the Stories

As we have said, this postmodern approach presumes that the research on a ministry project is by definition collaborative with a project design and reflection team. With others on the team, the leader/researcher initially takes a kenotic (self-emptied), curious, exploratory stance not only in the preparatory library and other research but also in facilitating the emergence and interpretation of participants' stories. It is also assumed that the leader's/researcher's family and life experience, education, religious outlook, value preferences, and professional journey will influence the telling and interpretation of the narratives, and should be owned and discussed throughout the project as needed.

Key to understanding the centrality of narrative in defining a faith community's realities is respect for the *powerful role of language in the construction of human experience*. John Winslade and Alison Carter say that "the differences between us are constructed in the metaphors and ways of speaking that we hold in common as language communities."[6] People in the world act upon their perceived differences from each other by constructing narratives that explain these differences and that organize their contextual experience. Language, and its defining metaphors, is the vehicle for the emerging narrative.

In evoking the *narrative of concern or opportunity* that is to be the focus of the project, the leader/researcher may well run into competing or conflicted interpretations that are being influenced by the self-defining narratives of the parties involved and the larger narratives with which they intersect. Though they may emerge around perceived opportunities for the

---

[6] John Winslade and Alison Cotter, "Moving from Problem Solving to Narrative Approaches in Mediation," in *Narrative Therapy in Practice: the Archaeology of Hope* (San Francisco: Jossey-Bass Publishers, 1997), 257

expansion and growth of ministries, these perceived differences may also be generating a *problem-saturated part of the story* that is causing pain, disharmony, negative projections, and lovelessness in various forms. Sometimes toxic story lines passed from generation to generation in a church, family, or other faith community can have a crippling or discouraging effect on ministry initiatives. These are encrusted parts of the faith community's story that have grown disproportionately influential in shaping a negative identity of the community. This can distort the mission and poison the brew of fellowship. Members' perceptions of each other and of the church can be also distorted, blocking action, creativity and spiritual nurture. However, it is essential to keep in mind that in postmodern thinking, "conflict is seen as malleable, not fixed, and emergent (changing as it emerges). There are different *versions* of meaning to be explored rather than a set of facts to be discovered."[7]

Collaborative deconstruction of these tangled stories and teasing apart the problem-saturated from the healthy and life-sustaining parts of the congregational narrative is an essential task that is augmented and supported by solid research as defined above. This discernment is enhanced through skillful use of *circular inquiry*. This mode of questioning of persons and data in a circular fashion to discover the circular and interconnected nature of human interactions has its origins in the family therapy theories of Boscolo, Cecchin, Hoffman, and Penn.[8] They discovered that the procedure they called "circular questioning" allowed families to function as an audience to each other, themselves, and the situations in which they found themselves. We believe it is also useful as a tool for narrative analysis in the study of congregations. Circular inquiry can help track through the congregation and community the common and disparate perceptions of reality and the ways in which distorted perceptions of difference perpetuate ignorance and block understanding and collaboration. In circular inquiry, the researcher

---

[7] Monk, *Narrative Therapy*, 255.

[8] Luigi Boscolo, *Milan Systemic Family Therapy: Conversations in Theory and Practice* (New York: Basic Books, 1987).

engages participants with a series of questions about the meaning of events as experienced by a number of persons in the community. For instance, the interviewer may learn from one participant that a church community is stiff and unfriendly, unwelcoming to strangers. The interviewer asks others about this and whether they have a similar or different perception. By evoking the concern or opportunity and tracking it around various persons who know about it, discerning the various meanings and interpretations surrounding the concern, a thicker, more elaborative story is likely to emerge. When this is accomplished, the emerging *preferred story* can be encouraged, supported, reflected upon, and given an increasingly available audience. This is a step towards a new, rewritten community story.

The sources of storied experience, though coded in a variety of ways, are vast and rich. Certainly foremost are face-to-face conversations in which the researcher engages with participants in the community. Some stories spill out naturally. Others are discretely hidden and must be sought after.

So, *intentional interviewing* is an integral part of the research effort. When people are encouraged to speak they not only report experience, they also reveal the meanings by which they have been formed as people and the relationships they have with each other. Moreover, when a variety of perceptions are shared in an atmosphere of caring and receptivity, the outlines of a shadow script, and possibly a preferred and more hopeful part of the story, may come to the fore.

Intentional interviewing provides a space for people to *notice and connect the storied meanings* that surface in their conversations and may not at first seem to have a connection. As in the example given previously, the putrid smells of effluent from a small town's collective septic systems may not at first seem to connect in a community's mind with political irresponsibility of town leaders in blocking the town's connection with a sewer trunk line. Nor might it seem a subject of theological concern, until a ministry research team connects the dots and the theological issue of the corruption of principalities and powers is raised, or biblical concern for the health and wholeness of all creation is brought into the conversation.

Clarifying the Theological Situation

Beginning a critical conversation between the stories that surround a ministry concern or opportunity, the ministry situation, and the faith tradition and theological grounding of the leader/researcher is essential to an effective beginning in Doctor of Ministry project design. Larger narratives that come into play are the theological tradition of the student's denomination, biblical and theological texts that have relevant bearing on the situation, and the experiential insights and knowledge of the ministry team. Theological analysis of the situation is intended to have a pervasive impact on the way the project is designed and the thesis is written. Interfacing the stories of conflict, dysfunction, and suffering with the stories of hope found in the Old and New Testaments constructs a roadbed down which the divine Spirit may choose to travel in order to touch and transform the situation. Through this form of discernment, alternative interpretations of shared stories can surface. A "plain sense" of the commonly held theological meaning of the ministry situation under study can emerge.

Evoking Research Stories That Intersect with the Situation

In addition to the *situational stories* harvested in the narrative research described above, there are other sources that help to flesh out the definition of a community's ministry concern or opportunity and augment and strengthen the ministry project. These are the *research stories* garnered from theological texts, social science, and the mining of found documents.

Theological reflection is generated by attention to the situation and to the leader's/ researcher's own story and tradition. The ministry concern or opportunity usually suggests further study of theological texts that expand the theory and scope of that reflection. Stories and story fragments are also to be found by opening the senses to written research findings that bear upon the concern or opportunity.

For instance, social analysis provides needed demographic information about the community context, such as its economic, ethnic, cultural, political, institutional and family structures. There are many guides for doing social analysis. Some of these resources are cited in chapter four.

Other social science resources, such as relevant research methods, instruments for measurement and evaluation, psychological theory, forms of political analysis, and tools for congregational study, may be suggested by the concern or opportunity itself. The research team should treat the ideas, meanings, and data gleaned from this research as story fragments that contribute to the understanding of a real or right story as gathered into the mutual perceptions of, and agreed upon by, the community.

Further, evoking the dimensions of the story, its plots, sub-plots, and "flesh," is not limited to personal conversation and reading scholarly texts. Found documents, reflections on group process, meeting notes, journals, histories, films, symbolic objects, church architecture, reports on congregational engagement with community, denominational, regional, or national issues, and other research sources, all contribute to discernment of the fuller defining narrative of the ministry setting and the influential narratives of participants and members. Similarly, documents such as minutes, sermons, legal proceedings; secondary theological sources such as confessions, books of worship, hymnals, rites and rituals; vision statements and educational curricula augment the research effort. Stories are also told in the music of the community and those who produce it. Crematories or grave sites surely tell a story, too. So do the many forms of play that cement community fellowship. Testimonies and confessions tell the story of a community's witness and its faith stance. Sensitivity to these intersecting multiple story fragments moves the research team closer to a plain or right sense of the community's story.

***

POSTMODERN NARRATIVE RESEARCH IN SUMMARY

Getting Started

So that the reader may take into the ministry research setting a simpler guide to the narrative research approach detailed in previous chapters, we have put together a summary below. While it is stated in a linear way, in practice this approach is usually messier and non-linear. Storytelling and story analysis are complex, variable, and unfold in unpredictable sequences and under usual and unusual circumstances. The story, if told and heard authentically, is more than two-dimensional. Still, we believe the summary might be useful to those who are new to the approach, so we present it here. The reader may wish to study the summary before moving on to the next section, which is an examination of a ministry situation demonstrating this approach.

Implementing the Approach:
Story Analysis in the Ministry Setting

Defining the Concern or Opportunity That
Prompts the Launching of the Project

The traditional research model seeks to isolate a clear, concise, one-sentence declaration of a specific problem in the practice of ministry that will become the focus of research and intervention on the part of the student. This thesis statement then becomes the central factor enabling the development of a case study. While retaining the need for establishing the boundaries of the project, the proposed new approach seeks to begin the process, not by identifying the location of a problem that needs resolution, but by evoking a conversation between the student and her/his ministerial setting that will lead to a mutual collaboration addressing the concerns of the participants and moving them to a new understanding and relationship that may affect a positive outcome. We begin, then, by suggesting a set of initial questions that will lead the Doctor of Ministry student to begin a conversation that will ultimately coalesce into the ministry project and thesis. Begin by asking questions such as: Why are you considering a ministry project? What is of concern to you, or to members of your ministerial context, in your ministerial setting? Why is it of concern? Hopefully these questions will begin the process of exploring the differences between interpretations of the current setting by the varying individuals and groups that participate in it.

Why Are You Considering a Ministry Project?

Why are we asking the student to begin focusing here rather than searching for problems to solve? One reason is that the authors believe this to be a somewhat less biased way of approaching one's congregation, ministry practice, or other ministerial setting. Rather than beginning from a search for dysfunction as compared to some sort of objective standard, from a problem, or from issue naming, one begins with a survey of what is present, without value-laden judgments of problem labeling. This awareness of "what is" will be further refined as the project continues to unfold, yet even at this nascent phase the participants have an intuitive understanding of the present condition. They may also have an interpretation of how the present condition of the ministerial context was brought about. That is, they will have a story concerning "how we got to 'what is.'" This is the starting point of the project: the "what is" and its interpretation by the participants. *Why* you are considering a project indicates that you sense a "difference" between "what is" and your expectation (or theirs) of "what could be" (the actual versus the preferred state).This is your area of concern or opportunity.

What Is of Concern to You, or to Members of Your Ministerial Context, in Your Ministerial Setting?

The project focus need not originate with the student. That is, the concern could be suggested by those in the ministerial context. The cry may be to "fix it." The job of the student is to differentiate between the content, the "what is," described as needing "fixing," and the *process*, the meaning, the understanding that the present is unsatisfying. So the area of concern is not simply a condition, but the interpretation of why the condition is a concern as well.

Clarify the Theological Situation That Prompts the Concern or Opportunity: Why Is This Concern or Opportunity Theologically Meaningful?

Begin a dialogue at the point of intersection of the current ministry narrative context and the biblical/theological story. How do you begin to think about your narrative of concern in terms of a larger narrative?

Establish a Safe and Comfortable Storytelling Environment with Inquirers

Join the conversation with warmth, self-differentiation, and non-reactive presence. Assume a kenotic, or self-emptied, attitude. Model respect, open conversation, reflection, and focus on meaning. Normalize and celebrate difference and frank discourse. Instead of facts, uncover narrative. Be aware of possible shadow scripts hinted at in the stories.

Make an open space to allow "sparkling moments" and "unique outcomes" to surface. These revealed story fragments tell of things that are dreamed of but not fully realized, hopeful events in the life of the faith community, and the lives of individual members, that function as mini-visions of a preferred future. Such moments or outcomes may be as simple but profound as the case of a timid but talented lay woman of our acquaintance who was encouraged and supported by her church board to lead what turned out to be a successful women's retreat, her first act of public leadership. The spread effect of this outcome to other potential leaders gave fresh energy and hope to their church.

Begin to assist participants by asking externalizing questions (questions that invite story-sharing about features of life and ministry not easily talked about in this particular faith community). This facilitates the unfolding of a thicker, truer story.

Invite Participants to Tell the Story, Focusing on the Faith Community's Narrative of Concern or Opportunity and the Ways Their Stories Interact with It (Awareness)

Recall that each telling is a new story and that each teller has an opportunity to be both teller and audience to her/his story. Listen for the variety of language forms, relationship patterns, meanings, legacies, polymorphic symbols, and the ways these have shaped the story.

Consult with Research Stories That Bear Upon the Concern or Opportunity

Student and research team introduce histories, leadership profiles, research findings, found documents, etc., into the reflection. Note content, concentrate on *relationship process within the faith community, tracing the interconnections of persons to persons, events to events, events to data and persons, and each of these to the whole.* Add depth, content, insight from research.

Map the Effect of the Narrative of Concern or Opportunity on Members and in the Wider Community

In conversation with participants, utilize circular inquiry. Begin to tease apart the story of concern from possible emerging elements for a new story. Compare, contrast, and evoke the fuller narrative. Inquire about differences and similarities of effects, and what influences what is heard. Focus on relationships, not problems. Encourage participants in the conversation to objectify the narrative of concern or opportunity as though it were another party to the conversation. Ask, "How has this concern or opportunity affected you, the church, and the community?" Or, "How would things be different if this concern or opportunity were not present?" Explore cultural/contextual dimensions. Track the effects of the dominant discourse surrounding the concern or opportunity on gender, power, cultural, and contextual features of congregational and community relationships.

Facilitate an Opening of Space for a
Preferred Story to Emerge (Hope)

Watch for hints or outlines of a preferred or altered story. Identify in the emerging narrative "sparkling moments" (eschatological moments) when things happened that are unusual to the narrative of concern or opportunity. Facilitate the interlacing of biblical narratives with the narrative of concern or opportunity. Deepen the content and meaning of this story by encouragement and creation of enactments of and wider support and audiences for the preferred story.

Re-imagine the Actualization of Faith: Coauthor and Develop the
New, Preferred Story with Participants (Transformation)

The preferred story emerges as a product of reflecting on and interlacing with the larger Christian/religious narratives that throw light on the problem of concern. It is an alternative story interpretation that points to "what could or should be" in contrast with the "what is" of the narrative of concern. Watch for the "plain sense" or "realness or rightness" that is in the emerging story. As the preferred story emerges, the leader's/researcher's task is to recruit ever wider audiences of those who embrace and support the emerging, preferred story.

For a graphic presentation of the above approach, refer to the figure on the following page:

LEARNING FROM THE STORY

The Ministry Contest

Uncovering the Narratives

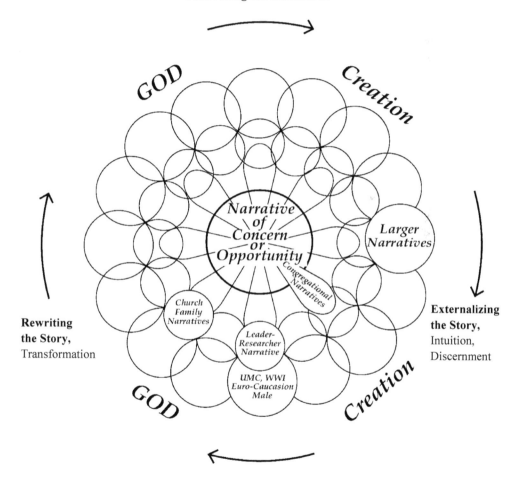

**Rewriting
the Story,**
Transformation

**Externalizing
the Story,**
Intuition,
Discernment

Deconstructing the Story,
Teasing Apart the Narrative of Concern
from the Preferred Story

APPLYING THE POSTMODERN RESEARCH
APPROACH TO A MINISTRY SITUATION

Learning from the Story

What does the approach we have previously detailed look like when a Doctor of Ministry student takes it in hand and puts it to use? The authors are fortunate that one of the students in Drew's Doctor of Ministry program (summer 2003) did just that. The Rev. Bonniekaren Mullen-Holtz has kindly granted us permission to use her initial narrative research and theological reflections on a difficult ministry situation, which would lead to her formation of a project topic outline. While it does not develop all of the facets of story analysis we have covered, we think it eloquently portrays the reflective process as we have described it. Here is her work in its entirety:[9]

DECONSTRUCTION OF THE STORY

****

Teasing Apart the Narrative of
Concern from the Preferred Story

"Rest in Peace"

When I was in my final year of seminary (LTSP) I found the days long and the rest little. When I needed rest and withdrawal, I would go to St. John's Lutheran (ELCA) Church located just yards from my condo. I assisted at St. John's so folks were used to seeing me there. St. John's has a

---

[9] Note that the student cited chapter numbers of this text from an earlier version. These have been removed by the authors to reflect the current version of the text.

cemetery in the back yard dating from the 1700s to the present. What was unusual, in hindsight, was that I would often on warm days go into the cemetery, tie up my dog and rest on the raised, horizontal headstones. It was the only times that I got to "rest in peace." Creepy? Frightening? Sacrilegious? Practical? Everyone got to weigh in his or her thoughts and even discuss it in some humor to this day.

The German "Boys"

During my time at St. John's, two friends of mine from Germany came to visit. We called them the German "boys." As was my custom for all visitors I took them to the cemetery to see some of the historic stones. At the end of the tour "the boys" were concerned. In Germany they said, only the most honored or historic graves are kept. Each grave is simply "rented" for a time. When the time is up the body is disposed of and a new "renter" takes the spot. Why would anyone keep a grave of a common person, they asked?

Land Locked

The Montgomery Square United Methodist Church in Montgomeryville, Pennsylvania is landlocked. The pie-shaped piece of land is bordered on two (2) sides by two (2) highways and on the third side is a Burger King. The church wants to grow, even go (somewhere else) but has a centuries-old cemetery on three (3) of the sides of the church building. Lying in the graveyard is the history of the church, the community, the state, and the nation. While the remains are dead, the history is alive. Periodically relatives knock on the church door looking for their ancestor's final resting place and in search of their own history. As you will see by the dialogue of church members and the pastor in Insert A, children often run through the cemetery, as though they are reliving Michael Jackson's video, "Thriller." Even adults, it is reported, walk carefully and measuredly past the stones, keeping tightly to the cement walkway.

The concern/problem for the church is what to do about the graves as they seek to move forward. The church wants to grow and has even voted to begin planning to grow. They have received an offer of $1.5 million for the property. It was joyfully reported that Babies-R-Us paid over a million dollars an acre for their land to the south of the church. However this price does not include keeping either living or dead inhabitants.

While there has been no open discussion, yet, there are murmurings. There are relatives of those in the cemetery among the congregants who have voiced concerns. There are friends buried there. There are soldiers from long ago wars. One stone says, "So and so died here. He fought in the War." You remember that War that was the War to end all wars. In this time of war, do we want to disenfranchise or dismiss those of the past who made the ultimate sacrifice? These are the emotional concerns. Is the church to throw out the old to bring in the new? Where will "grandma" finally rest in peace?

Let's be honest; there is a financial consideration as well. It will cost $1,000 per grave for the graves to be moved. Who knows just how many folks lie in each grave from long ago? The unnamed and unknown might reside there as well. There are legalities to who knows and for how much in filing expenses and possibly legal expenses. $1.5 million dollars could be gone just resolving the cemetery issue.

"The Soul of a Man"

"There is no such thing as a soul," declares theologian Nancy Murphey of Fuller Theological Seminary. Hank Hanegraff, best known as the *Bible Answer Man*, asks, "If there is a general resurrection but no immaterial soul, how then do you retain personal identity? How does the same human being, having died, rise again as the same person?" These are just a few of the arguments among theologians about the theological and philosophical argument of "the soul."

While theologians might enjoy the intellectual challenge, what does the laity do? If there is no separate soul, does it stay with the body—in its grave? Is "grandma" and her "soul" lying just outside the church windows listening to her favorite hymns, watching over her grandchildren? Where will the supposedly active soul or essence or spirit of "grandma" go if she is moved? The cemetery has become the high place for this church and many other churches.

Identifying a Problem/Opportunity

Herein lays [sic] the practical, historical, communal and theological problem/opportunity. What does Montgomery Square or any church do when it believes that its growth potential or lack of potential is dependent upon the living *and* the dead? Further, how will the laying out of this issue bring about resolution? Could it divide the church where division does not yet seem to exist? We would hope it would only be the beginning of a frank and potential-filled discussion, but information and survey can only bring on dialogue, not control it.

"[A]dvocate for a method of theological communication in which the discourse 'seizes' the *imagination* of the people and transports them from their current thought and imaginal world to another, with transformative results."[10] How will this issue contribute to the theological growth or lack of growth of the congregation? Upon reflection I see that this could become, if I may use the word, simply a theological concern that corporate insight might lead to a material resolution that will not divide the church but also not free or direct the church body towards theological insight.

The Process and the Protocol

It was the pastor of the Montgomery Square church who originally brought up this subject to become a project topic. He had left an embattled church four (4) years ago and does not want a supplementary battle in this church. Yet he is aware that the church cannot remain static. This gives the entrée to the Third Step of the Theological Reflection. The church is on the verge of growth having heard God's voice of mission to the "others." The

---

[10] See Chapter 2, p. 57.

appropriate committees have raised the capital. Monies for a land purchase will soon be changing hands for 10 acres a few miles away. The next step is to sell the church property and start building the new church. Though they have heard God's voice about mission, they have not yet heard God's voice of the theological why, but have muffled it with the excitement of doing.

The group I have chosen to be on my committee includes six lay members and two clergy. There are Lutherans (one a former Roman Catholic), one former Roman Catholic and now a United Methodist, and four life-long United Methodists. The two Lutheran participants have already dealt with this concern/opportunity at their own church. The stories of the two Lutheran members will be included in the final product. For them there was church plant structure change and physical growth, but there really was no resolution of either the theological or cemetery site difficulties.

To begin this paper I presented a number of stories. Montgomery Square is not the only church with this concern/problem in Montgomery County. There are others, in this church and others, with stories to tell, to be elicited and surveyed. The research that will be coming through this project will include as many churches and persons as is controllable and fruitful to give us appropriate material for Critical Thinking (Chapter 2). However childish it might appear, I have to confess that I would never have stayed in that cemetery at St. John's at night! I need to reflect, as well, on my own story, the second step in theological reflection (Chapter 2). So concerned with the living, I have not been able to see beyond the act of dying and the resurrection of all the saints on the Last Day. I fear that I fear that among the dead there is no God and that around those that have died there abides a living energy that has no good in it. I must be careful that I don't just collect a lot of ghost stories in the theatre of the macabre.

The pre-cognition to our study is the recognition that God is present and will continue to be talking through the Word and Sacraments and Community and through the people's stories. An initial cursory library search has already brought forth other's stories. In just the inviting of my team, I have had six stories and an initial theological reflection, which I believe, will grow deeper in time. It appears that we will need time to find

the commonalties of the theological language we will be using. In
choosing religious diversity, it appears that I am the only one who, over
the years, is familiar with and has used many faith languages. Our own
resolution of the language to be used will be a story in and of itself. The
precursor to our study is also the recognition that God is already speaking
to the people and through the people of Montgomery Square United
Methodist Church and that we can only illuminate not translate their
stories.

> But the traveler needs a map, however poor it may be, to
> find his or her way. Michael Christensen's map for
> theological reflection on spiritual pilgrimage and ministry
> involves the theologian's mystical apprehension of divine
> revelation, discerned through intuition centered on the heart,
> faithfully applied in following the vision of three streams
> from the divine Source—Father, Son, and Holy Spirit—
> realized in Worship, Community, and Mission.[11]

> Another map, one created for theological reflection on
> modern evangelism, comes from the work of Professor
> Leonard Sweet. In his model, or map, he employs the
> discernment and appropriation of contemporary images as
> his hermeneutical principle, citing their capacity to evoke
> spiritual response, transformation and change.[12]

In reading this I am focusing on the use of the word "map." It will be
a map of the cemetery, both historically and physically that, I believe, will
initially attract our participants, but it will be the map which is created of
the congregation that will be of utmost importance in the end. Will this

---

[11] Michael J. Christensen and Carl E. Savage, *Equipping the Saints:
Mobilizing Laity for Ministry* (Nashville: Abingdon, 2000), 161.

[12] See Chapter 2, p. 62.

"new geography" be able to support the "new land" of change and growth they say they desire?

"Our Town"

Do you remember the play "Our Town"?[13] If you don't, I will give you a brief synopsis. The entire play is shown from the viewpoint of the "citizens" of the local cemetery that sits on a hill overlooking the town. The "dead" comment and reflect all during the play of the happenings in their hometown. As new "citizens" joined the ensemble, more stories were elicited of life with all its struggles and joys and finally upon death, with its joys, struggles, losses and gains. "Our Town" was about stories, noting that every life had a story that intersected and veered all along the way until its supposed conclusion and repose in the cemetery overlooking their hometown. Reflecting on Chapter 3, we can see every story as part of the "Our Town" story. The community of believers, wherever they reside, becomes "Our Town." Every story tells of the intersection and veering off of the experience of life. No story can possibly be the same and behind every story are many other stories.

"Imagine There's No Heaven . . ."

The John Lennon song "Imagine" asks us to imagine that there can be a world so different than what is; that there be no heaven, no hell, to imagine there is only earth below us, and above us only sky, just to imagine a world so different, so pure, so free, not meant only for the Dreamer. You can call this change transformation, plain sense, realness, or rightness. What we can only do through this project is to make an offer for the people to "imagine." To imagine themselves as the whole people of God, to become what God would have them become, to hear all of God's words and will for them in Word, Sacrament, and Community. Hopefully,

---

[13] .Thornton Wilder and Robert J. Lee, *Our Tow: A Play in Three Acts*, illus. Robert J. Lee (Avon, Conn.: Limited Editions Club, 1974).

we will hear all the people of God, in and through all their stories, culminate in a united "Amen!"

**

Crafting a Topic Outline

The student cited above has done some fine preliminary work on her ministry project, particularly attentive to utilizing the first two phases of the postmodern narrative approach with skill and integrity. At first she is guided by anecdotal conversations and other available information circulating in this community concerning the disposition of gravesites that lie in the pathway of proposed community development. A preliminary focus has been suggested by this input and confirmed by more intentional story gathering from the ministry situation. She obtains narratives from visitors (cultural stories), lay advisory committee members, church members, relatives of the dead, and developers. She brings in some reflections on the local, national, and international history (larger narratives) embodied in the cemetery. She puzzles about the unfolding story of the church's stewardship, mission, and future goals. She makes some theological connections between her personal experience with graves and gravesites, with several biblical/theological notions about death, the afterlife, and the resurrection.

In short, she familiarizes herself with all of the available narratives that intersect with the ministry situation and begins a theological/critical dialogue with them. The definition of her project and the direction her research will surface out of this dialogue.

This student is ready to take the next step, which is putting together a topic outline. The topic outline is a beginning blueprint for the project and the thesis that will issue from it. The topic outline, once approved by faculty, is expanded by the candidate into a full-blown project blueprint, the prospectus.

The topic outline has a title for the project, the student's name, the date it was written, the statement of concern or opportunity that prompts the project, the purpose of the project, theological connections to the project, the scope of the project (its context, its limits), definitions of important terms used to describe and elaborate on the project, and a preliminary bibliography citing sources to be pursued.

While acknowledging that this student might put together a Topic Outline in a number of different ways, the authors present one possible version below.

***

TOPIC OUTLINE

"Rest in Peace: Creating a Structured Narrative/Theological Dialogue among Citizens of Montgomeryville, Pennsylvania to Guide the Disposition of Beloved Gravesites"

Narrative of Concern/Opportunity

The Montgomery Square United Methodist Church in Montgomeryville, Pennsylvania is landlocked. The pie-shaped piece of land is bordered on two sides by two highways and on the third side is a Burger King. The church wants to grow, even go (somewhere else) but has a centuries-old cemetery on three sides of the church building. Lying in the graveyard is the history of the church, the community, the state, and the nation. While the remains are dead, the history is alive. Periodically, relatives knock on the church door looking for their ancestor's final resting place and in search of their own history. Children often run through the cemetery, as though they are reliving Michael Jackson's video, "Thriller." Even adults, it is reported, walk carefully and measuredly past the stones, keeping tightly to the cement walkway.

The concern for the church is what to do about the graves as they seek to move forward. The church wants to grow and has even voted to begin planning to grow. They have received an offer of $1.5 million for the property. It was joyfully reported that Babies-R-Us paid over a million dollars an acre for their land to the south of the church. However this price does not include keeping either living or dead inhabitants.

Herein lies the practical, historical, communal and theological concern/opportunity. What does Montgomery Square or any church do when it believes that its growth potential or lack of potential is dependent upon the living and the dead? Further, how will the laying out of this issue bring about resolution? Could it divide the church where division does not yet seem to exist? We would hope it would only be the beginning of a frank and potential-filled discussion, but information and survey can only bring on dialogue, not control it.

Purpose of the Project

The purpose of this project is to create a structured Narrative/Theological Dialogue among the citizens of Montgomeryville, Pennsylvania to guide the disposition of beloved gravesites situated on property owned by Montgomery Square United Methodist Church. The candidate and a chosen laity team, utilizing a Postmodern Narrative Research approach and instructed by the biblically-based practice of church-yard burial as a metaphor for the communion of saints (such as Genesis 50, Ezekiel 37) and biblical teachings on the resurrection of the dead (such as Matt. 27, John 11, John 5:28), will design and implement a series of structured dialogue sessions. The goal of these sessions will be to evoke stories from the parties in the community and beyond the community that intersect with the church's concern for the disposition of the gravesites. After study and narrative analysis of these stories a theological/reflective summary and report will be made available to the church's membership and leaders as a study document and guide to future mission planning. The intent is that they may imagine themselves as the whole people of God, to become what God would have them become, to hear all of God's words and will for them in Word, Sacrament, and Community. Our hope is that, in the spirit of "Our Town" we will hear all the people of God, in and through all their stories, come together in a united "Amen!"

Scope of the Project

The project will be limited to the parish area surrounding Montgomery Square United Methodist Church in Montgomeryville, Pennsylvania. However, stories will be gathered from available relatives of those buried there, from town, county, and Judicatory officials, and from other churches and leaders who have faced similar dilemmas. Research narratives gleaned from reading books, journals, found documents, and the contemporary discourse around death, being, and spirituality discovered in films, music, and other expressions of popular culture will also be incorporated. The project will be designed to take place within a time frame of December through March, 2005. It will also consider carefully the optimal dates and times for gathering and listening, and the reasonable amount of time necessary to process and reflect on the mass of material harvested from the stories.

Definitions

Postmodern Era—An emerging socio-cultural era beginning roughly in the 1950s and extending to the present, characterized by a relativizing of truth, values, and meaning; suspicion of absolute truths; rejection of deterministic claims of science; focus on language and societal discourse (story) as formative of reality and selfhood; celebration of diversity; and acceptance of the social construction of guiding cultural norms.

Narrative Method—A research tool developed by social scientists that requires the researcher to be emptied of preconceived notions and prejudices, curious investigator of the stories of contemporary people. Narrative method is intended to make research more unbiased, inclusive, and attentive to the uninterpreted meanings and truths latent in the stories.

Bibliography

Atwood, Joan D., ed. *Family Scripts*. Washington, DC: Accelerated Development Press, 1996.

Bandy, Thomas G. *Facing Reality: A Tool for Congregational Mission Assessment*. Nashville: Abingdon, 2001.

Barnes, Elizabeth. *The Story of Discipleship: Christ, Humanity, and Church in Narrative Perspective*. Nashville: Abingdon, 1995.

Elliot, Robert, ed. *Environmental Ethics*. Oxford: Oxford University Press, 1995.

Friedman, Edwin. *Generation to Generation: Family Process in Church and Synagogue*. New York: Guilford Press, 1985.

Friedman, Edwin, Edward W. Beal, and Margaret W. Treadwell, eds. *A Failure of Nerve: Leadership in the Age of the Quick Fix*, An Edited Manuscript. Bethesda, MD: Edwin Friedman Estate/Trust, 1999.

Grenz, Stanley J. *A Primer on Postmodernism*. Grand Rapids, MI: Eerdmans, 1996.

Holland, Joe, and Peter Henriot. *Social Analysis: Linking Faith and Justice*. Maryknoll, NY: Orbis Books, 1983.

Presnell, William, Carl Savage, and Michael Christensen. "Ministry in a Postmodern Context." Photocopy, Doctor of Ministry Department, Drew University, Madison.

Robson, Colin. *Real World Research: A Resource for Social Scientists and Practitioner-Researchers*. Malden, MA: Blackwell Publishers, 2002.

Steere, David A. *Spiritual Presence in Psychotherapy: A Guide for Caregivers*. New York: Brunner/Mazel, 1997.

Steinke, Peter. *Healthy Congregations: A Systems Approach*. Bethesda, MD: Alban Institute, 1996.

Stevens, Paul R., and Phil Collins. *The Equipping Pastor: A Systems Approach to Congregational Leadership*. Washington, DC: Alban Institute, 1993.

Woodward, James, Stephen Pattison, and John Patton, eds. *The Blackwell Reader in Pastoral and Practical Theology*. Malden, MA: Blackwell Publishers, 2000.

✳✳✳

Once the topic outline is approved by faculty, the student is free to develop it into a full prospectus. Guidance for this next step is outlined more fully in the *Drew University Doctor of Ministry Manual*. However, in the next chapter we will present the reader with some practical methods and means that must be considered in the development of a prospectus and then pursued in the execution of any ministry project.

CHAPTER 4

Methods and Means

The surface of the earth is soft and impressible by the feet of men; and so with the paths which the mind travels. How worn and dusty, then, must be the highways of the world, how deep the ruts of tradition and conformity![1]

—Henry David Thoreau

A century ago, as the numerous wagon trains left Saint Joseph, Missouri, for the trek across the plains already rutted by the tracks of earlier wagons, the eager pioneers read this sobering message on a banner across the western end of the main street: "Choose your rut carefully. You may be in it all the way to California!"[2]

---

[1] Henry David Thoreau, *The Writings of Henry David Thoreau*, ed. Bradford Torrey and F. B. Sanborn (Boston and New York: Houghton, Mifflin and Company, 1968), 356.

[2] There are many variants of this "choose your ruts" proverb. This version from Eddie Levick, "It Takes Guts to Get Out of the Ruts," Moment of Meditation, http://www.mcba.com/Action/Devotion.nsf/ a161246e35e1e46b86256449007474e6/50d7cf36e212809f862567f6000e3798?Op enDocument.

Albert Einstein was once asked how he worked. He
thought about it for a moment and then said with a smile,
"I grope."[3]

***

Since the contemporary American church is situated within a society that is being transformed by a diversity of world civilizations, it is essential that we offer our best to the study of faith communities and use the tools of social science and theology effectively.

So far we have offered the postmodern narrative approach as a new way to conduct research on ministry sites and the multiple contexts in which they are nestled. We feel that by choosing the narrative metaphor as a means to understanding the discourse of communities of faith and the meanings that are organized and communicated in this discourse, we come closer to discerning the immediate impact the Spirit may be having on these communities. Thus, we prompt the leader/researcher to gather stories from the context itself, that is from participants, leaders, the researcher's own life, the faith community's denominational tradition, and the lore and history of the faith community and its surrounding context.

Yet, there are other kinds of narratives that might bring insight to reflection on the narrative of concern/opportunity at the ministry site. These narratives are the yield of research methods that researchers choose as tools for organizing broad-based inquiry into the ministry context. The

---

[3] Sam Horn, *That's Original: Don't Repeat Clichés; Re-Arrange Them!* (2003), http://www.nsaspeaker.org/information/mag/May05ThatsOriginal.shtml. The I grope comment may be somewhat of an urban myth, but Einstein did say in a more formal setting when asked about how he arrived at the special theory of relativity: "There is, of course, no logical way leading to the establishment of a theory but only groping constructive attempts by careful considerations of factual knowledge."Statement sent to a special meeting of the Cleveland Physical Society, 19 December 1952, honoring the centenary of Michelson's birth; printed in R. S. Shankland, "Michelson-Morley Experiment," *American Journal of Physics* 32 (1964): 16–35.

field is vast, and our task in this presentation will be limited. Examples of appropriate research methods are the more comprehensive approaches to social analysis (Holland and Henriot); Systems relationship analysis (Bowen, Friedman); the Congregational Studies model of Bandy; or the electronic programs for contextual assessment of congregations available in cyberspace such as Faith Communities Today, initiated at Hartford Seminary. These are described below. The leader/researcher might use these as a means of uncovering social structures and functioning, relationship process and patterns, demographics, language and discourse, and other powerful influences on the concern/opportunity under study.

More modest and practical research tools often used in Doctor of Ministry projects are focus group formats, pre- and post-project questionnaires, Likert scales and checklists, behavioral observation and analysis, forms for participant feedback narratives, leadership assessments with evaluative criteria, and so on.[4]

In addition to the methods cited above, narratives that intersect with and illumine the concern/opportunity also may unfold from research stories garnered from books, documents, films, and other studies. We reiterate here that the findings from the forms of research discussed above are themselves narratives, subject to the same theological and critical engagement as other stories. For those who have, with others, tended to look to the findings of structured social science research in the form of case studies, psychological or sociological studies, learned books, monographs, and journal articles as more reliable and "objective" avenues to the truth, we sound a loud caution. These are valuable means to understanding, but they all embody the particular world view, philosophical biases, and parochial outlook of their authors that may create a constricted vision just like other means of understanding ministries. Most of all, they tend to avoid reflection on the processes and meanings of the situations studied, and instead emphasize "facts" and "data."

---

[4] Colin Robson, *Real World Research: A Resource for Social Scientists and Practitioner-Researchers* (Cambridge, MA: Blackwell, 1993).

Research Methods

As we consider models and methods for ministry research it will be helpful for us to think together for a moment about Myers' thoughts on the possible kinds of research that practice seems to recommend as most useful for Doctor of Ministry research projects. Myers observes that there are three research approaches, which we will now examine.[5]

The Quantitative Method

This method strives for objectivity and control of variables. It seeks to develop and prove or disprove stated hypotheses with research outcomes. Its findings are validated or disputed by exact replicas of the study by others. This is difficult at best even for trained social scientists and is not recommended for Doctor of Ministry projects. However, even with the Case Study Model, which is more useful for Doctor of Ministry research, quantitative methods such as questionnaires, check lists, and other data-gathering instruments, can flesh out, or thicken, the case story. Also, it is valuable for a researcher in any field to consider the outcome of comparing at least two alternative and separate sources or approaches to a research problem, opportunity, or concern with one's own findings. Such a triangle of sources tends to yield more objective findings and avoid myopic focus on one's own preferred ideas or theories.

The Qualitative Methods

Ethnographic Research Method—Using this method, the researcher becomes a "participant observer," joining the faith community as a kenotic, or empty, listener. It is not that the researcher's ideas or experience are useless. It is that our own biased perceptions are likely to rush us towards hasty interpretations of the stories we are hearing unless we make an intentional effort to prevent it. So, we attempt to maintain an unbiased, kenotic position in order to understand the culture of the faith

---

[5] Myers, *Research in Ministry*.

community. Locating and engaging with "hosts and hubs," gatekeepers, key informants, and found documents are among the research activities of the participant observer. So is the examination of artifacts, symbols, rituals, and language. The researcher's personal reflections in the form of journals, process notes, field notes, and verbatim accounts of relationship encounters are valuable data for ethnographic study of ministry sites.

Proactive Research Method—Here the researcher makes no pretense at objectivity, though every attempt is made to be open to the unfolding story of the research culture, and to avoid imposing an unfit or objectionable agenda upon it. Ethnographic methods may still be useful in such research. However, with the proactive methods the leader/researcher joins the culture proactively, with the intention of deliberately working toward an identified, agreed-upon agenda for change. The goal of proactive research is not only understanding but transformation. The actions of all participants are evaluated, including those of the researcher.

None of the models for social analysis presented below can be considered quantitative methods. Holland and Henriot's model should be seen as a proactive method, primarily because it launches from a specific theological stance (Liberation Theology informed by Roman Catholic tradition), and seeks transformation of social structures and patterns through the active use of research findings to influence changes towards peace and justice, and advocacy for the poor and underprivileged.[6]

Bowen methodology, an offspring of Bowen Family Therapy Theory, is also a proactive method that seeks to identify the systemic structures and relationship process of the research culture by joining it like a social science observer, but maintaining a "systems expert" position in the system. Objectivity is sought through the assumption of the role of the self-differentiated leader/researcher who is able to maintain a clear, intellectually determined stance and not be overwhelmed by the emotional pressures and homeostatic patterns of the system. However, in most cases,

---

[6] Joe Holland and Peter Henriot, *Social Analysis: Linking Faith and Justice* (Maryknoll, NY: Dove Communications Orbis Books, 1984).

the leader/researcher does use her/his unique position in the system to deliberately influence the system towards needed changes identified by informed and cooperative systems analysis.

The postmodern narrative approach may also be considered a methodological approach, with roots in postmodern narrative philosophy, narrative theology, and narrative family therapy. However, it forsakes attempts at objectivity by taking instead a kenotic, or emptied, approach and assuming that the leader's/researcher's own story (culture, tradition, personal family history, era, etc.) is but one of a host of narratives that are intersecting and influencing a current ministry setting. Broader cultural traditions are studied, but not as authoritative insight into the present. Truth claims of scientific methods are suspect, since such methods are founded on certain philosophical generalizations and shaped by the discourse and power alignments of the dominant society. As the researcher guides the examination of the research community's stories and studies them, their contextual reality "bubbles up" to give the researcher a fleeting snapshot of the multiple influences that surround the problem or concern/opportunity. This inclusive character of the Postmodern Narrative Research Approach positions it to be an umbrella methodology, under which can be gathered a host of intersecting research findings (narratives) gleaned from a variety of research methods that bear upon the concern or opportunity under study in the ministry context. The researcher does not presume in advance that specific changes are needed. Rather than assume the role of change agent the leader/researcher facilitates the uncovering of the "problem-saturated" part of the ministry site's narrative, evokes and helps tease apart the story of concern or opportunity from the emerging "preferred" story, and joins with the community as it "rewrites" its story under the influence of the Spirit.

Some Useful Models and Methods

Social Analysis Model of Holland and Henriot

These authors presume that civilizations evolve from simpler to more complex community order over time. Along with this development come more elaborate social structures (family, business, church, law, education, etc.) whose purpose is to facilitate the life and welfare of its citizens. This model supposes that evil can be and often is ensconced in social institutions and social behavioral patterns that oppress those with less power in the social system. Social analysis assists the proactive leader/researcher in the task of uncovering these and seeking creative, transformative change.

Holland and Henriot put forth a paradigm for how an historic succession of perspectives (Traditional, Liberal, and Radical) for understanding society and social conflict and change can be summarized for the use of social analysts.[7] They say that a key ingredient in social analysis is grasping, from a particular perspective, how its adherents perceive a social system's governing principle, underlying metaphor, and view of time, social space, and conflict.

Holland and Henriot propose that, historically, western culture has been variously influenced in its social development by three culturally ensconced models of change: The Traditional Model, the Liberal Model, and the Radical Model. By applying these in social analysis the researcher can draw general conclusions about the history, structure, and societal behavior of the research universe under study.[8] A second paradigm for social analysis, say these authors, equips the social researcher to assess the impact on the research universe of competing aspects of social development, such as economic, social, and political development.[9]

---

[7] Holland and Henriot, *Social Analysis*, 32. 152

[8] See Holland and Henriot, *Social Analysis*, Chapter 2.

[9] See Holland and Henriot, *Social Analysis*, Chapter 3.

These authors show how the Roman Catholic Church has responded to three distinct stages of industrial capitalism over an extended period of history. In this way, the reader is presented with one distinct way of reflecting theologically on social process, drawing theological conclusions, and implementing ministries based on those conclusions.[10] Theological reflection is integrated with this model in at least two ways. One is its strong ties to the values and theological principles of Liberation Theology. The other is in the authors' guiding schematic for social analysis, which is a circle of movement from Insertion to Social Analysis, to Theological Reflection, to Pastoral Planning.

Finally, Holland and Henriot recommend to the reader several models for social analysis.[11] Students are urged to familiarize themselves with these models.

Bowen Family Systems Theory and Other Systems Theorists

Murray Bowen's Family Systems Theory springs from the basic systems idea that a group of interrelated parts, plus the way they function together, compose an identifiable system.[12] When applied to humans and their social relationships, the systemically generated emotional process in each relationship configuration—couple, family, church, or other organization—functions in exactly the same way. Concepts originally developed by Bowen are: the differentiation of self from family of origin patterns; emotional triangles; emotional cutoff; family projection process; sibling position; multigenerational transmission process; and societal emotional process.[13]

------

[10] See Holland and Henriot, *Social Analysis*, Chapter 4

[11] See Holland and Henriot, *Social Analysis*, Afterword.

[12] Michael Nichols and Richard Schwartz, *Family Therapy: Concepts and Methods*, 5th ed. (Boston: Allyn and Bacon, 2001), 104.

[13] Michael Kerr and Murray Bowen, *Family Evaluation: An Approach Based on Bowen Theory* (New York: Norton, 1988), 13.

Virginia Satir, a pioneer in the application of communications theory to family dynamics, added to systems thinking the notion that all relationship systems have common, definable components. These components are defined as *parts* (parents, siblings, extended family, each with a role to play); *structure* (variable and invariable behavioral sequences and patterns, rules for order and change); *purpose* (guiding mission, relationship contract or covenant); *communication patterns*; and *links with society.* [14]

Finally, scholar-practitioners Imber-Black, Roberts, and Whiting have deepened our grasp of the transmission of family culture within and across generations through their study of the way meaning is embodied and communicated in human relationship systems through rituals. In any relationship system, large or small, rituals convey meanings that can contribute to the functional health or dysfunction of that system, especially when they broker multigenerational family or corporate patterns of behavior.[15]

When used as a research method, systems analysis often provides valuable insights into the underlying meaning of interactions among people by looking at the influence of family of origin and intergenerational relationship patterns. Then the researcher can determine their impact on a given concern or opportunity for ministry. The tools of systems analysis enable the researcher to analyze and better understand the emotional process of people in relationship.

According to Nichols and Schwartz, some important intellectual forbearers of systems theory are Bateson, Bertalanffy, Haley, and Weiner.[16] These early explorers studied the application of Cybernetic, General

---

[14] Virginia Satir, *The New Peoplemaking* (Mountain View, CA: Science and Behavior Books, 1988), 131.

[15] Evan Imber-Black, Janine Roberts, and Richard Alva Whiting, *Rituals in Families and Family Therapy* (New York: W.W. Norton, 1988).

[16] Michael P.Nichols and Richard C Schwartz, *Family Therapy: Concepts and Methods* (Boston:Allyn and Bacon, 2001.

Systems, and Communications Theories to social systems. Systems theory also draws upon the structural/functional sociological theory of Talcott Parsons,[17] whose theory provided a view of families and other social organizations that included their defined systemic and sub-systemic parts, clear boundaries, the mutual influence of parts and whole, and role definitions of members.[18] This holistic thinking was a strong influence on Murray Bowen and his theory. But Bowen, following General Systems Theory, stressed our emotional and biological similarity with other creatures, especially in brain functioning. And he drew conclusions from observation of the bio-social relationship structures of living creatures.

The metaphorical connection of the Church as the body of Christ with the systems thinking of Bowen and others is keen. Theologians tend to think of human beings as whole in the relation of mind body-spirit. The Church is one body, with individual parts interrelated in its whole functioning.

Systems as a Metaphor

Family Systems is but one expression of the systems metaphor. Reality in systems thinking can be summarized as follows: Reality is intentional; we know that even viruses have an uncanny intentionality in their systemic functioning. Reality is relational; the *systemic causality* of symptoms in relationships is a guiding principle. Each part of a family or social/institutional relationship system acts upon and is acted upon by all of the other parts. Each part influences the whole, as in the variable patterns observed in a kaleidoscope when it is moved. Reality is storied; our lived reality is the multigenerational story of self in relationship to self,

---

[17] See for example Talcott Parsons, *The Social System.* (New York London: The Free Press Collier-Macmillan Ltd., 1964) or Talcott Parsons and Robert Freed Bales, *Family Socialization and Interaction Process* (Glencoe, Ill.: Free Press, 1954).

[18] Nichols and Schwartz, *Family Therapy Concepts and Methods*, chapter 4.

world, others, and God in systemic interaction and mutual influence. In fact, reality is composed of the interaction of one agent acting upon another and each part upon the whole, with a transformational result.

Systems Analysis of Relationship Systems

Seeing all relationship systems by means of an eco-systemic metaphor applied in Systems Theory can be useful in the analysis of families and other social systems. For instance, the local church is a relationship system that operates under the same order as all other relationship systems.

Systems are best understood through a study of their intergenerational stories. These stories portray systemic forces of togetherness and separateness, me and we, self regard and loss of self and increased anxiety.

The anxiety referred to in systems theory is not the emotional tension usually observed in "up tight" people. Nor is it the same as the normal tension of everyday life. Anxiety pervades the organism and registers its presence even at the organism's cellular level. Anxiety is the organism's "flight or fight" reaction to destabilizing threats, large and small. When people in relationship systems experience these threats they seek to "bind," or contain, the resultant anxiety by such behaviors as controlling others, clinging to or blindly following leaders, and indulging in addictive conduct or conflicted relationships. Most anxiety is unconscious and is observed in faulty relationship patterns, blaming or denial, or outbursts of buried fear and misery. It is also something that binds people together. When intensified by stress and conflict, anxiety tends to prompt emotional regression in the system, is chronic in institutions such as churches, and can be expressed in outward ways that belie the blind reactivity that drives it. Reactivity and intolerance of difference are indicators of systemic anxiety worsened by emotional fusion, poor differentiation of self, and anxious reaction to chronic or currently intrusive stressors. *The nature of emotional systems* is to exhibit anxious reactivity and polarization under stress. These stress triggers can be understood in systems. So can the influential role of family of origin patterns of participants and historical patterns of dysfunction of the system itself that bear down on relationships in the present and exacerbate reaction to stress.

Homeostasis and *morphogenesis* are terms that refer to systemic change. Homeostasis is the tendency of a system to remain the same and stable.

Morphogenesis is the complimentary tendency of systems to elaborate and change (reorganize) to accommodate systemic pressures.[19] Resistance to change insinuates itself in the presence of *holons*, which are regulatory patterns established in the systems to help the system remain stable.[20]

Systems concepts can be useful to the study of faith communities. *In faith communities there are typical conflicts, puzzlements, and problems on which systems analysis can throw light.* These are usually leadership issues or congregational issues.

Leadership Issues

One of these problem areas arises with the arrival of a new leader to a faith community. When people come or go for any reason, a system usually reacts with increased anxiety. Or, a faith community can suffer a mismatch in the fit of clergy and congregation. In this case it is not unusual for passive or active sabotage of leadership to occur. Furthermore, even when an established leader introduces significant changes or leads in charismatic ways, sabotage of that leader or the leader's agenda is not uncommon, even on the brink of success. System anxiety (as in the form of fear of change or loss of control) kicks in automatically. Only systems-perceptive and self-differentiated leaders can anticipate this and deal successfully with the resistance of the system. However, at a given time in

---

[19] Nichols and Schwartz, 115.

[20] The reader can find a more extensive discussion of Family Systems Theory in Michael E. Kerr and Murray Bowen, *Family Evaluation an Approach Based on Bowen Theory* (New York: Norton, 1988).

the life of a congregation, deft movement between varying styles of leadership on the part of a pastoral leader may contribute to the healthy functioning of the church system. Leadership styles may be consensus, charismatic, or self-differentiated. Friedman[21] and Collins and Stevens[22] say each of these styles has its place in the effectiveness of system leaders. Leaders may assume any of these at any time to suit circumstances and system realities. Consensus leadership can lead to the tyranny of the weakest. Or, if a leader is charismatic, she/he may get too far ahead of the community on their mutual journey towards change and invite sabotage of agreed upon goals. Self-differentiated leaders recognize that they can only change their position and relationship behavior as leaders and use that position to influence change.

Fuzzy functional and systemic leadership roles can also create dysfunction in a faith community. For example, laity can function as clergy without credentials and thus avoid accountability, leading to confusion and sometimes abuses of power. Smaller churches with a histories of part-time and/or ineffective professional leaders and untrained lay leaders are especially vulnerable to these leadership conflicts.

When leaders focus on the *content*, the "what happens," of interactions rather than their *process*, the meaning of what happens, they often misjudge situations of conflict.

Congregational Issues

Alternatively, a new minister can be easily inducted into regularized destructive relationship patterns of a faith community to its designated clergy leaders. These patterns might be old, existing triangles, disputes

---

[21] Edwin Friedman, *Generation to Generation: Family Process in Church and Synagogue*, Guilford Family Therapy Series (New York: Guilford Press, 1985), 224–30.

[22] R. Paul Stevens and Phil Collins, *The Equipping Pastor: A Systems Approach to Congregational Leadership* (Washington, DC: Alban Institute, 1993), 58.

between families, tensions between Church School and Christian Education Committee, conflicts and power struggles between Trustees and Administrative Boards, and so on.

Attention to the systemic features of a faith community may help to identify and bring relief to painful symptoms of systemic dysfunction. The following is a list of features that may typically be present: a congregation might be fused with other systems, such as church agencies or local businesses; systems may be either closed and rigid or open and flexible (the closed system does not deal with change well}; the system does not grieve for its losses, is fearful of its family secrets; system rules, defined in books of order or in codified common practices of the faith community, may be ambiguous or poorly understood and administered; congregations can be traumatized by recent experience, be polarized, and appear as anxious, controlling, or paralyzed; and, members may exhibit post-traumatic stress symptoms, left over from social disruptions or catastrophes or from the anguish of local political wars.

Other realities of a given relationship system can spawn or perpetuate dysfunction. Difficulty in maintaining appropriate boundaries may also be a problem or concern for faith communities. This usually indicates poor self-differentiation, inadequate relationship covenants or agreements, or vague or unenforced system rules. When a system's founding promises are poorly negotiated and its rules fuzzy, or when its expectations are covert, not open (such as a lack of clarity about the professional staff's salary, days off, space, manse, insurance coverage, study leaves and continuing education funds), system anxiety reactivity increases.

Old losses and memories can invade and exacerbate new crises and losses, for example with the displacement of anger, etc. Legacy binding may also occur when loyalty to past leaders or cherished memories of "the way things used to be" cloud the church's vision. Triangles among members, leadership, and the issues that separate them may become stressed and cause dysfunction. Typical ones are: staff and issue; staff, parishioners, and issue; minister, board, and family; layperson, minister, and ministry functions.

Self-differentiated leaders/researchers are those who are able to join the system and occupy a position from which to influence the system. They will keep the needs of self and others in balance, take a clear, intellectually determined stance, and will not be overwhelmed by the emotional pressures and homeostatic patterns of the system. Self-differentiated leaders focus less on the *content*, the "what happens," of interactions and more on their *process*, the meaning of what happens. Poorly differentiated leaders often misjudge situations of conflict. Take, for example, the situation of an elderly parishioner who has just told you that it is "perfectly o.k." that a memorial painting, dedicated to her long departed son, be removed from the altar and placed in the fellowship hall of the church. She then departs sobbing, and slams the door. The "o.k." is the content of the interaction; the sobs and door slamming are the process, or meaning, of the interaction.

Self-differentiated leaders persist in staying connected to all persons in the system, including those with whom they are in conflict. This reflects to others the leader's self-awareness, courage, and emotional maturity and allows the leader to maintain self-boundaries in difficult, stressful situations. Self-differentiated leaders understand their own family of origin patterns, including their position in their family birth order, and how these impact and how they impact their leadership and other relationships. Finally, mature and self-differentiated leaders coach others towards differentiation, as well. They model appropriate leadership styles and systemic relationship skills.

Systems Thinking and Theology

Steere has contributed valuable theological insight into the discussion of systems and theology. In his book *Spiritual Presence in Psychotherapy*, he provides the reader with a framework for understanding how the Divine Presence is manifested in the relationship process of human beings as they live out their situations in life. The seeker's quest, spurred on by spiritual hunger and spiritual homelessness, leads to varied attempts to discern the nature of humankind, acquire a sensible view of creation, and gain knowledge, however intuitive or grounded in religious experience, of how the divine presence is made known to human creatures.

One of these "windows" into divine presence, says Steere, is a systemic model.[23] Driven by a perception of causality that is systemic rather than linear, systems thinking promotes the idea of levels of intelligence, all part of an evolving, ever-changing whole, in which one level of intelligence communicates with and is influenced by every other. Life is thus regulated by a "watchful intelligence" of self-correcting circuits that operate to keep life in balance. Aggregate experience passed on from generation to generation in the form of recurring patterns, beliefs, etc., means that the good and the bad of experience are shared and often replicated. However, this homeostasis is interrupted by the need for change and elaboration, and is, at the fruitful moment, interrupted by the wrenching and straining of the system.

Steere asserts that the human mind and consciousness are limited, so we cannot fully fathom the whole of the Mind of God, the total consciousness of all that is. Thus our relationships and decisions are flawed by limitation and our failure to comply with the wisdom of the whole, with the ecology of divine creation. As far as the Godhead is concerned, systemic thinking is comfortable with the Trinity, since it is a metaphorical way to explain divine presence in three aspects of expression, none of which is complete without the rest.

Wisdom, in systems thinking, is living life in growing awareness of the whole of creation and its systemic order and process. Humility and self-differentiation, in which one claims and tends to one's own process and behavior and forsakes imposing her/his will on others, is a key to spiritual growth. Discipleship is a partnership with the divine in which we discovery what new thing from God is breaking through, and join with it.

---

[23] David A. Steere, *Spiritual Presence in Psychotherapy: A Guide for Caregivers* (New York: Brunner/Mazel, 1997), 219–40.

Other Tools for the Study and Analysis of Faith Communities

Bandy's Congregational Mission Assessment Tools

Bandy's approach to the study of congregations brings together a variety of tools designed to collect information and identify perspectives about a congregation, its context, and its leadership.[24] It is aimed at stimulating congregations to break out of familiar patterns of church life in which they are stuck and claim a more dynamic, missional stance for the twenty-first century that reflects current realities.[25] Bandy provides leadership and congregational worksheets, surveys, and analytical direction. One product of the approach is a comprehensive congregational profile.

Faith Communities Today

Leaders/Researchers might consult this remarkable resource described below to find out more about congregations across denominations and faith groups as well as to discover social science resources for the study of their own congregations and community religious contexts. Below is the introduction to the web site (http://www.fact.hartsem.edu/) on which this information is available for free:

> *Faith Communities Today* is the largest survey of congregations ever conducted in the United States. It is the most inclusive, officially sanctioned program of interfaith cooperation. The project was initiated to enhance the capacity of participating faith groups to conduct and use

---

[24] Thomas G. Bandy, *Facing Reality: A Tool for Congregational Mission Assessment* (Nashville: Abingdon, 2001).

[25] A CD version of the book is included along with the hard copy.

congregational research. This study is intended to provide
a public profile of the heart and soul of religion in
America—local congregations—at the beginning of a new
millennium.

In addition to the above resources the leader/researcher is directed to
the numerous web sites which pop up by typing in the search,
"Congregational Studies." These sites provide bibliographies, research
tools, and a plethora of information about the study of congregations.

CHAPTER 5

Evaluation in Postmodern Ministry Research

" 'Well done' does not mean 'all done'."

—Len Sweet[1]

In a way it is ironic that at the moment you crystallize the discovery, you disengage from the process of discovery. And yet, evaluation is a very necessary part of research. Unless we at some point disengage from the ongoing practice of ministry, we may fall prey to only hearing our own voice, our own narrative, and lose the transcendent. The evaluation process enables us to step back from an instrumental use of reason to control something that "works" and to reflect on the presence of the divine unfolding. It is necessary at times to retreat from the actualization of faith in a practice of ministry in order to re-imagine the story and to listen again to the narratives of context.

In terms of the approach we have set forth in this book, the purpose of evaluation for us differs from one that merely organizes the data or presents the findings. There are two parts to our notion of evaluation: observing change and discerning transformation. As previously we

---

[1] These words were sent to the "Postmodern Quartet," a group of four of the Dean's Fellows who were collaborating on their Doctor of Ministry project as part of the initial online group of the Drew Doctor of Ministry Program. They had completed their projects but were not revising their papers.

employed analyses of varied types to de-confuse the context, we now employ techniques of evaluation to represent that context in its new intersection with the narratives of participants, surrounding external groups, tradition, and biblical story. This evaluation emphasizes the aspect of storytelling that is informative, but as we know, in its telling story may also be transformative to the reader as well.

We see a form of evaluation that consists of two distinct parts. One part is observing change. This first part is fairly straight forward; you compare the state of the context prior to a new ministry intervention and afterward. In a sense, this part of evaluation is only a measurement process. Has there been change in activity, habits, stories told, etc.?

The second part is discerning transformation. The definition of transformation is "a marked change, as in appearance or character, usually for the better."[2] The latter part of this definition is critical in this understanding of the purpose of evaluation—discerning transformation toward a preferred future.

Transformation refers to a change in structure, appearance or character—"for the better." Assessing these kinds of change is at the heart of the evaluation of ministry projects. However, we can imagine what a slippery slope this can be! In this chapter we will suggest perspectives on transformation that could help to thicken the evaluation story without squeezing the project story into a paradigmatic mold. This perspectival approach[3] to evaluation envisions the ministry project story as a diamond with many facets. In order to appreciate the diamond's holistic beauty one must either turn the diamond slowly or encircle it, so that the refracted light of the Spirit can shine into our eyes from each facet to enlighten us. We suggest below that we alternate among five different positions around

---

[2] *The American Heritage Dictionary of the English Language.* (Boston: Houghton Mifflin, 2000).

[3] We are indebted to Seward Hiltner for this image. See his book, *Preface to Pastoral Theology.* (New York: Abingdon Press, 1958).

the diamond, to fully sense the project story and come closer to understanding the "gem" in all of its beauty.

We need to remind ourselves again that the process we are engaged in utilizes discernment in lieu of measurement. We do not propose that we can measure transformation on an absolute scale, although we may perhaps be able to employ some objective tools to measure changes in some aspects of behavior, attitude, or condition. But often the growth or modification we seek to make certain has no equivalent benchmark with which to match up. Nor, even if it existed, would such a one dimensional appraisal be sufficient. We wish to assess a future now become a present newly arisen from the past we had analyzed. This new dynamic situation has in part come about not only from the stimulus of the project but also in the interaction of the complex dynamics that encompass the ministerial context. We have not worked in a controlled laboratory, nor have we worked on inanimate material. Thus, we are not detailing experimental results.

Instead, we describe the new orientation to the realities present at the end of the process that sought to empower a preferred future. We may ask: What is the Spirit doing? What is emerging? What has been called forth? (Lazarus come out . . .) Again, this is discernment and not measurement. The future that has now become the present is a condition, not an inevitable state. Each present moment of experience is defined by its past, or future, or both. You have moved your ministry perspective from a "now" to a new "now"; from one emerging future to another. The preferred story is future as preferred relationships.

We also need to be aware that change does not unambiguously connect to progress. Change is not progress; it is simply change. Therefore, the emphasis on process is now as equally important as in the beginning stages during which the student uncovered the narratives surrounding the context. The evaluation process includes researcher and partners, all participants, and the project itself. It is a narrative that has realized that the effects are emergent and not straightforwardly causal from the project; therefore the standards for evaluation are conversant and not brought ready-made to the discussion and imposed on the experience. Not all the partners may be of the same mind regarding the project's influence, but there is, hopefully, a consensus that the earlier process of reflection and action has created a preferred path of realization.

The evaluation as we envision it is focused on new meaning and not "truth." That is, the evaluation is tentative, provisional, and modest. One should always be aware that "nothing gets solved for very long." However positive or negative emotions surrounding the experience of the project may be, the evaluation is not simply based upon the "feel good" aspect of the project. Ultimately, one seeks to assess what tools or skills were imparted, what new relationships were forged, what systemic changes occurred that will affect the future of the context beyond the newly established condition. We are more interested in the web of relationships and the growth of the participants individually, or the context collectively, than in a mere change of condition. The project was not treating a "disease" but a "patient" and so the evaluation should continue the process of examining the whole story and not just an abstraction from it.

Thus, hopefully, the narrative of evaluation portrays what may be valuable for others in their ministry practice. It should avoid generalizations, but seek to specifically comment on the experience from within the context. It should allow others outside of the specific faith community to hear for themselves the conversation of the ministry context. As one was kenotically listening at the outset, now one narrates not advertises; one announces not propagandizes. That does not mean one should not be embolden to state where one has been made wise by research, inspired by the emergent outcome, or surprised by grace. These too are valuable components of the total experience to be shared. The evaluation process is not limited to the intended outcomes, it is not reportage of experimental results—it is a portrayal of a ministry practice that others may wish to incorporate into their own. Consequently, it is necessary to fully portray all the complex of actions, ideas and relationships that were exchanged and developed in the course of the project so that the reader can match theory-stories against observation-narratives. This is necessary so that one can be fully aware of the intricate framework of the ministry context and the experience empowered in the course of the project.

For that reason, all aspects of the project must be considered when engaged in the process of evaluation: the clarification of the theological situation, the captured "sparkling moments" of transformation, the limitations and illusions faced.

A great beginning place for evaluating ministry projects is to note social change in any of the three major constituents for the project (context, team, and leader/researcher). One should even begin by asking if there has been consensual social recognition of transition. In other words, did anyone notice a difference? This is important whether the change was incorporated or conflict remained. Either result indicates that the project was engaged by those involved in ways that intertwined with the prior narratives of the dynamics of the context.

Since postmodern evaluation seeks to understand changes in the ways faith communities identify themselves and practice that identity, altered boundaries and/or worldview of the ministry context, the team or the student are important signals. The change in identity or conditions may indicate that the preferred story is entangling the ongoing story of the context and stimulating a change in relationships and structure that may harbinger its emergence. There are at least five perspectives to choose from for this evaluation.[4]

These perspectives assist the researcher in discerning and articulating the "thickened" story emerging from the project's contexts. Typical ways of examining the renewed post-project context include functionalist, ecological, materialist, structuralist, and semiotic perspectives. These perspectives enable one to examine any transition in identity or social interaction and to assess the "realness" or "rightness" of the conclusion of the project. Identity includes the boundaries and worldview of the context,

---

[4] These perspectives are first developed by Robert Schreiter as ways of listening to a culture in his work on local theology. He details how local theology develops from the encounter with stimulus from the larger culture. See, Robert J. Schreiter, *Constructing Local Theologies* (Maryknoll, N.Y.: Orbis Books, 1985).

the team, and the student. As each of these three were affected by the process, so a change in any can be studied to determine the value of the project and its impact.

Looking more closely at the perspectives that may be employed in evaluation, we turn first to how functionalist evaluation might examine how the combining narratives of the context fit together pre-and post-project. This perspective seeks to discern how parts of a context might fit together differently now. It builds on the sense that if one component system is changed, that change affects the whole. While this perspective can be used in a deterministic way, it also allows for the researcher to discern "unintended" consequences that may have emerged by the programmed initiatives.

Traditionally, the ecological approach is employed when determining how a society relates to its physical environment. In our approach to understanding a specific context in its larger context, we may move this understanding of ecology beyond a simple physical basis. That is, the ecology of a ministerial context does indeed incorporate its relationship to the physical environment, but we may include its relationship to other larger cultural contexts. These larger contexts function perhaps as the physical landscape in which the ministerial context resides. Take, for example, a local church that is located in an urban area. The urban physical landscape is the physical environment that the ministerial context relates to on one level, and one can move outward to the global environment from that starting point. But the local church also relates to other larger contexts that could also be construed as its ecological environment. For instance, the denomination that a congregation participates in could be a larger context. Thus one could discern if there has been a change in how the ministerial context, the team, or the researcher relate to these larger entities.

The materialist perspective closely resembles the previous perspective except in one important dimension. While the ecological perspective looks at how the context relates to the larger environment, the materialist perspective looks at how the context is affected by changes in the surrounding environment.

The larger environment can affect the context, the team or the researcher's worldview, and needs and responses to social change. Thus in employing this approach one would look at factors "beyond control" that impinged during the project implementation phase and their discerned influence on the emergent story.

The structuralist approach looks for unconscious patterns that may shape the context. This may have remained unobserved during the development phases of the project, when narratives were being listened to and a project was being proposed, only to come to the fore as resistive elements to the changing of the story of the future of the context, team or researcher. The post-project structure may instead be an emerging structure. New patterns arise to replace old ones, or new textures are applied to old patterns. By examining these, one can gain a renewed sense of the identity of the context as it exists and perhaps gain insight toward unforeseen barriers to the emergence of a preferred story.

The semiotic approach examines the images, messages, codes and metaphors that express meaning for the context. The approach relies heavily on descriptions of that context from within (*emic*) or from without (*etic*) the context. It is likely that the researcher will, as participant within the context, be able to discern only from inside the narratives that affirm the identity of the group. However, it may be possible to examine narratives explaining and analyzing the experience of the context from the outside, comparing the experience of the group from a similar cultural setting. One could examine the context's intended message of concern to that of the message that is related meaningfully to the larger cultural setting; the spoken story to the heard story.

Whether one or more of these perspectives is employed is secondary to the goal of obtaining a holistic sense of the emergence of the new within the ministerial context. The key is to encounter the developments engendered by the project's stimulus and/or by changes in the larger narrative context of the culture. This encounter may lead the researcher to affirm, modify or correct the pre-project discernment as well as to uncover forgotten or avoided parts of the local narratives. The hope is to stimulate further positive developments in the emergence of a preferred future.

Evaluation of the "Rest in Peace" Project

Having laid down some theoretical guidance above, we now turn to the question of how the Narrative Research for Ministry evaluation process might work if applied to the work of student leader/researcher. We will focus on the project concerning the disposition of a church graveyard from chapter three. Remember that all evaluation is ongoing, and that theological insights and meaningful turns in the emerging story must be monitored while the project unfolds and not only at its completion. But in our hypothetical construction of the project we cannot supply all the complex voices that we might have heard in an actual project context. That "thickened" story would surface only as the work of reflecting on the narratives intersecting with this concern proceeded in the real context. We acknowledge that that fuller story of the disposition of these church gravesites has not emerged in "real life" as yet. Thus we can only discuss below the possible directions that evaluation of this project might take.

When we have completed a research project a natural question pops predictably into mind: Did the project succeed? That is, did it meet the specifications written into the project proposal? That answer is spelled out in a context-specific evaluation narrative, a subjective composition of discernment, intuition, and reflective nuance. The evaluation story is the researcher's attempt to display on the screen of the reader's consciousness a representation of the content, process, and perceived outcome of the project.

The leader/researcher's purpose, as stated in the Topic Outline, was to "...create a structured Narrative/Theological Dialogue among the citizens of Montgomeryville, Pennsylvania to guide the disposition of beloved gravesites situated on property owned by St. John's Lutheran (ECLA) church." In addressing the question of whether or not the project succeeded in its purpose we first look at what happened to implement the project.

We start with a general observation: The researcher places concern for the whole community at the forefront of the research effort. She accomplished this by imagining the project as the creation of a meeting place where stories surrounding the history, meaning, and eventual disposition of beloved grave sites could be heard and understood by any who chose to participate. Even in the initial gathering of the actual intersecting stories from various community and personal sources, she demonstrated her conviction that the resolution of the concern was potentially in the story telling and listening of the community.

The diversity of the voices that she awakened in her solicitation of stories is impressive. There are stories from the young men (the "German Boys") whose culturally defined lower regard for the permanence of graves contrasted with the higher regard of the Montgomeryville people. There is the demographic story that details changes in the surrounding community that have forced the church and its graves to relocate. The Lay Advisory Committee is composed of clergy and laity, some of whom who have already experienced the same event at other churches where they have previously been. They have a story to add to the present discussion from these prior contexts.

Relevant biblical narratives were interlaced with the concern by the researcher. This biblical wisdom provided insight into the ways earlier faith communities have considered burial. One prevalent image from the biblical narrative that she lifted up showed that the church yard was seen by some early interpreters as metaphorical for the communion of saints. In general she treated death and burial praxis in the light of a theology of the resurrection of the dead. The leader/researcher also introduced a larger research narrative, citing theologians on the theological issues surrounding the survival of the soul after death and at the resurrection of the dead.

Stories were mined from church members, whose stake in the preservation of the graves was high, as well as from books, journals, and other documents that portray contemporary discourse around death, being, and spirituality. Judicatory officials from the leader/researcher's United Methodist faith tradition provided yet another larger narrative of theology and practice to engage with the narrative of concern. The research team benefited from the research stories of systems and social analyses. This wide reach for stories to include in the research bodes well for the project.

The Leader as Story Broker

The effectiveness of the project was also gauged in part by noting how the leader/researcher handled the above stories. She was able to identify the dominant cultural discourse around death and the meaning of life and perceive its possible role in arresting initiatives to talk about, reflect on, or resolve the concern. She took a kenotic, or emptied stance as she listened. She worked with her team to fashion a safe and comfortable storytelling environment. She saw commonalities and differences among the stories. She facilitated the teasing apart of the "stuck" or problematic features of the story of concern from a possible emergent, more hopeful story.

Hints of an emerging story in this faith community's struggle with the graveyard come from the leader/researcher's appropriation of two images. One image is from "Our Town", where the stories of the living and the dead are all connected, all significant. Wherever they reside in the houses or in burial yard of the town, these remembered ones belong to the community of faith. Her approximation of this connection in her context through the project is of significance.

A second image that the leader/researcher introduces is that of the utopian community from John Lennon's "Imagine There's No Heaven". This image has the potential to abduct the consciousness of this faith community. Through it they may be helped to imagine a very different future, not one without heaven, but one in which they freely "imagine themselves as the whole people of God" having listened to all of God's words through Word, Sacrament, and Community. Having done that, they may find a "real and right" way to proceed in moving their church's location while preserving the dignity of their honored dead.

The leader/researcher's own told story prepared her to listen. It awakened shadow parts of her past graveyard experiences as well as her thoughtful, mature sentiments and hopes for the transformation of her faith community. She claimed her fear as a part of her story. This may have had the effect of sensitizing her to the fears of other storytellers, thus freeing them and her of unnecessary fearful inhibitions. The *Thriller* image she identified is a symbolic way of describing the barely conscious apprehension of many contemporary people that if they do not run fast enough from death and its "spooky" aura it will surely catch up to them in short order. The image may have been more effective than words in alerting participants to their possible captivity to such fears. The leader/researcher was aware that she and her team could start, but not control the sharing of stories surrounding a graveyard. Graveyard stories are part of a socially conditioned wariness of powerful forces at work under the surface of consciousness when people touch upon the subject of mortality.

Methods and Means

The leader/researcher followed up on her stated intention, and utilized the tools of social analysis to flesh out the story of the context. She had already described some of the demographics in her statement of her narrative of concern.. But discovering the nuances about the concern that were particular to various cultural or racial groups in the community thickened the story. Understanding the local political structure was an essential ingredient for the decisions the church will eventually make about selling the church property and disposing of the graveyard in some fashion. For instance, zoning and environmental laws will need to be followed and bureaucratic channels opened in order for disposition of the graves to proceed. Tools of social analysis help the research team to better understand their community's world view, outlook on change, preferred use of human space, relationship to the environment, and other critical matters which will influence how they deal with the gravesite.

This student also proposed using systems analysis to develop an intersecting narrative that would thicken the research story. How thoroughly she understands systems thinking and the skill she shows in using it is one element in the evaluation of this project. Systems thinking would predict that the prospect of moving both the church and gravesite would raise community anxiety and might lead to polarizing interactions among people of varying views. By joining this system with compassion, understanding, and tolerance, the leader/researcher could use whatever leadership position she has in the emotional process of the wider community to influence communication towards the desired issue-focused dialogue. She would be equipped to notice how attitudes towards death, burial practice, and memorializing the dead are transmitted across generations through recurring patterns of social interaction, including ritual behavior that conveys their meaning. Her grasp of systems would instruct her self-differentiated leadership, which could be expressed in calm, non-reactive presence at the meetings, staying connected to those who might differ with her leadership choices, and de-triangling with those who would draw her unnecessarily into controversy. She and the laity team could also raise alternative ways of thinking about the graveyard, presenting options to those whose myopic outlook keeps them from seeing more than one way to move from problem to solution.

Most of all, perhaps, is the reality that this church system and the wider systems that interlock with it, are in a transition period of great significance for the future. Systems must elaborate and change when the established relationship patterns and interrelating parts are overwhelmed with additional demand, lest they decline into dysfunction. The old ways of coping and maintaining homeostasis in this faith community are not working because the physical and social forms that sustain stability are rapidly changing. Transformation must take place or the church may lose its opportunity to develop itself further, enable new, awaiting ministries, and rise to the challenges of a new location. These systemic realities seem very much on the mind of the leader/researcher and her team, and this may empower them to act. Montgomeryville UMC could die and be buried where it is, or be resurrected into new life, with a rewritten story co-authored with the Spirit.

Transformation

We now turn from describing the project implementation and the measuring of change to the discernment of transformation. To do this we turn to our five perspectives: functionalist, ecological, materialist, structuralist, and semiotic. In the following paragraphs we become more hypothetical than above where we assumed how the project impacted the context.

If we were to look at the Montgomeryville UMC project story through the functionalist perspective we would ask how the pre-project aggregate of surrounding stories differs from the ways the stories come together post-project. Before the project it would seem that there were unheard voices, such as those of relatives of the buried dead, town officials frustrated at the slow pace in disposing of the graves, townspeople whose stories would eventually release some of their fears and surface sentiments that could lead to solutions, traditionalists whose minds could not bend towards impending change, and faithful persons across denominations whose theological outlook prevented the considerations of certain options for the continuing the honoring the dead than reposing in the church graveyard in its present location. At the end of the project's dialogue sessions, did any of this change? Was there a growing sense of direction, a surfacing of commonality of enlightened intuition and sentiment that hinted that a "real and right" direction was on the horizon? In the team's promulgation of a document that captures an emergent, re-written story, were there positive responses, reversals of polarized positions, a new confluence of storied insight that might point the way to a new future for the town and the church?

Or, if we were to view the project from the ecological perspective, we would ask were there changes in the way in which the church, the ministry team, or the researcher related to larger contexts that impinged upon the project? In this case, how did the legal establishment of state and county institutions influence the emerging gravesite story? Did dealing with these agencies around the moving of graves, or of effects of traffic patterns on the value of the church property, etc., fix or expand any ways of thinking about their help or hindrance in the minds of participants? Were any new ways of relating forged, for good or ill, with the United Methodist agencies whose policies had to be considered in the church's relocation? Did the cross-denominational conversation designed into the project effect any hopeful perceptions of future ecumenical cooperation?

From a materialist perspective, one looks at the pre and post perceptions of project participants of their church's identity and the difference attributable to perceived changes in the physical environment of the ministry context. The church was once located on a sleepy country road. Then, it was captured between busy parallel roadways. For those with memories that span the two conditions, has this project helped them deal with the painfulness of lost fond memories as well as connected them with the current realities and possibilities for honoring the saints of the past while affirming ministry in a new location? Or, for those who saw the moving of graves as desecration, has the project transmuted their consciousness of the sacred to consider optional ways to respectfully and faithfully remember their forbears?

Moving to the structuralist perspective, what changes occurred in initially unconscious, but later manifested resistances observed in participants dealing with death and burial, struggling with their honest beliefs about the meaning of life, death, and afterlife, and accepting permanent changes? Part of these changes would be forced upon the community by way of the church's decisions. Did the story-telling design of the project open up safe opportunities for people to voice their fears and beliefs? Was old community business and history sorted out from the current situation? Was the projection of past negative relationship patterns of citizens with each other confronted? Did this issue in any new awareness? Did they go away from the dialogue sessions with renewed hope for better community relations? And were the ideas of townspeople, church members, and project participants received and considered, leading to a new sense of being heard, and perhaps a changed consciousness of what could be? Did the team employ their knowledge of this social system and system dynamics, and use circular inquiry and other narrative methodology to help externalize a more complete story and name any emerging patterns?

Finally, from the semiotic perspective this project offers some potent images and coded messages, which convey contextual meaning. One cannot miss the symbolism of graves surrounding the church on three sides. The church is encompassed by a cloud of witnesses to the history of their faith, their community, state, and nation. These dead ones have seen and experienced all of it. But the symbolism is also one of constriction and crowding. Roadways bordering the church close it off and bring the noise, smell, and debris of modern society to the footsteps of the church. The nearby Burger King is an alternative community meeting place to the church fellowship hall. Food service is fast there, and the only obligation is to pay. Anyone is welcome. Have these important but coded messages been discerned and their meaning lifted up in the dialogue sessions and research discoveries of the project? Has this made a difference? One could look for one of the outcomes of this project to be creative ideas for the relocation of the graves. An example of such re-imagining by a church was described by another Doctor of Ministry student. In a situation similar to that of Montgomeryville UMC, his church decided to use part of the proceeds from the sale of the former church property and with permission exhumed the remains of those buried in the churchyard. As large wing to a new church, the congregation designed and constructed a memorial chapel surrounded by burial crypts holding the relocated remains. Information about each person relocated to this new place was researched and made available in memorial books at the chapel. In the new chapel were held all manner of worship services, not just funerals but also weddings, youth worship, and baptisms. The symbolic meaning was not hard to discern: in God's house no one is forgotten or turned away.

The members of the Montgomeryville church are at a nexus where the story of their concern over church relocation and disposition of gravesites, crosses with the story of their opportunity of a re-imagined future. Can the church find a course of action which will propel them into a future burgeoning with promise, hope, and new ministries in their new location? The evaluation narrative that is written at the project's close may well disclose the answer.

Final Remarks

We stated previously, a story intends a future. Recognition of what has happened can lead to the possibility of re-imagining and affecting what is to come. Our narrative approach's aim is to express the meaning held in the "what is" of the present configuration of the many intersecting narratives of a faith community and to explore the concerns and opportunities embedded within that community. We observe changes in conditions and discern transformations and changes in identity. We seek to entangle the local story of faith again, consciously, intentionally, with a plain sense of the story given to us by God.

This is a dynamic process that may lead to affirmation, modification or correction of previously held myths and parables that describe our understanding of reality. The preferred future may emerge from the collaboration of our speaking and listening to God directly and to God through each other. Together we hope transformation, that change for the better, takes place.

***

Afterword[1]

This book defines a Narrative for Ministry approach that values the place and importance of story. We understand that Story is a natural element for Native American culture. Within the context of educating Native American students, we have discovered that Story-telling is both informative and transformative.

This approach gives value to listening within a cultural context without comparison to another perspective. We feel that this is an important insight that will serve all persons within a specific cultural context.

We believe that such contextualization will provide an atmosphere in which one can discover, in conversation with others, the work of God in our midst. Such discovery brings meaning to the cultural context and to the individuals who seek such conversation within the sharing or Story.

This book makes the point that one cannot lead without first becoming a meaningful participant in the common life. Such participation can be developed by involvement in the conversation and sharing the Story through the act of listening within specific cultural context. When time is taken to listen within this context the approach values the uncovering of forgotten or avoided parts of the local narratives. The result can be a sense of seeking from within the people which leads to the incorporation of those in the emergence of a preferred future.

---

[1] From the original Indian University Press publication of Narrative Research in Ministry in 2005.

We recommend this approach and look forward to its integration into the life of our College as it seeks to be faithful to its historic education mission of education with Native Americans.

Chief Kelly Haney   *Rev. Dr. Robert J. Duncan, Jr.*

Principal Chief Seminole Nation   President
Master Native American Artist   Associate Professor of Religion
Former Oklahoma State Senator   Bacone College
United Methodist Pastor Bacone
College Alumnus and
Director of the Capital Campaign

Bibliography

Atwood, Joan D. "Social Construction Theory and Therapy Assumptions." In *Family Scripts*, edited by Joan D. Atwood, 12–22. Washington, DC: Accelerated Development, 1996.

Bandy, Thomas G. *Facing Reality: A Tool for Congregational Mission Assessment*. Nashville: Abingdon, 2001.

Barnes, Elizabeth B. *The Story of Discipleship: Christ, Humanity, and Church in Narrative Perspective*. Nashville: Abingdon, 1995.

Bateson, Gregory. *Mind and Nature a Necessary Unity*. Advances in Systems Theory, Complexity, and the Human Sciences. Cresskill, N.J.: Hampton Press, 2002.

_____. *Steps to an Ecology of Mind*. Chicago: University of Chicago Press, 2000.

Berger, Peter L., and Thomas Luckman. "The Dehumanized World." In *The Truth About the Truth: De-Confusing and Re-Constructing the Postmodern World*, edited by Walt Anderson, 36-39. A New Consciousness Reader. New York: Putnam, 1995.

Boisen, Anton T. *The Exploration of the Inner World: A Study of Mental Disorder and Religious Experience*. Chicago: Willett, Clark & Company, 1936.

Boscolo, Luigi. *Milan Systemic Family Therapy: Conversations in Theory and Practice*. New York: Basic Books, 1987.

Browning, Don S. A *Fundamental Practical Theology: Descriptive and Strategic Proposals*. Minneapolis: Fortress Press, 1991.

_____. "Pastoral Theology in a Pluralistic Age." In *The Blackwell Reader in Pastoral and Practical Theology*, edited by James Woodward, Stephen Pattison, and John Patton, 89-103. Malden, MA: Blackwell Publishers, 2000.

Chambers, John. "The Corporatization of Ongoing Education." *Trend Letter* 19 (5 October 2000): 2.

Christensen, Michael J., and Carl E. Savage, eds. *Equipping the Saints: Mobilizing Laity for Ministry.* Nashville: Abingdon, 2000.

Clinebell, Howard, *Basic Types of Pastoral Care and Counseling.* Nashville: Abingdon, 1984.

Ebert, Roger. *"Secrets of Pulp Fiction."* May 1995. http://www.godamongdirectors.com/tarantino/ faq/secrets.html.

Foreman, Rowland, Jeff Jones, and Bruce Miller. *The Leadership Baton: An Intentional Strategy for Developing Leaders in Your Church.* Grand Rapids, Mich.: Zondervan, 2004.

Foucault, Michel. "Nietzsche, Genealogy, History." In *Language, Counter-Memory, Practice Selected Essays and Interviews*, 139-64. Ithaca, N.Y.: Cornell University Press, 1977.

Frei, Hans W. *Theology and Narrative: Selected Essays*. Edited by George Hunsinger and William C. Placher. New York: Oxford University Press, 1993.

Friedman, Edwin. *Generation to Generation: Family Process in Church and Synagogue.* Guilford Family Therapy Series. New York: Guilford Press, 1985.

Geisler, Norman L., and Ronald M. Brooks. *Come, Let Us Reason: An Introduction to Logical Thinking.* Grand Rapids, MI: Baker Book House, 1990.

George, Carl F. and Warren Bird. *Nine Keys to Effective Small Group Leadership: How Lay Leaders Can Establish Dynamic and Healthy Cells, Classes, or Teams*. Mansfield, Penn.: Kingdom Publishing, 1997.

Gerkin, Charles V. *Widening the Horizons: Pastoral Responses to a Fragmented Society*. Philadelphia: Westminster Press, 1986.

Grenz, Stanley J. *A Primer on Postmodernism.* Grand Rapids, MI: Eerdmans, 1996.

Hiltner, Seward. "The Meaning and Importance of Pastoral Theology." In *The Blackwell Reader in Pastoral and Practical Theology*, edited by James Woodward, Stephen Pattison, and John Patton, 27-48. Malden, MA: Blackwell Publishers, 2000.

_____. *Preface to Pastoral Theology*. New York: Abingdon, 1958.

Holland, Joe, and Peter Henriot. *Social Analysis: Linking Faith and Justice*. Maryknoll, NY: Orbis Books, 1983.

Hopewell, James F. *Congregation Stories and Structures*. Philadelphia: Fortress Press, 1987.

Horn, Sam. "That's Original: Don't Repeat Clichés; Re-Arrange Them!" 2003. http://www.nsaspeaker.org/information/mag/ May05ThatsOriginal.shtml.

Huff, Darrell. *How to Lie with Statistics*. New York: Norton, 1954.

Imber-Black, Evan, Janine Roberts, and Richard Alva Whiting. *Rituals in Families and Family Therapy*. New York: Norton, 1988.

Jennings Jr., T. W., "Pastoral Theological Methodology." In *Dictionary of Pastoral Care and Counseling*, ed. Rodney J. Hunter, 862 864. Nashville: Abingdon, 1990.

Keller, Catherine. *Apocalypse Now and Then: A Feminist Guide to the End of the World*. Boston: Beacon Press, 1996.

Kerr, Michael, and Murray Bowen. *Family Evaluation: An Approach Based on Bowen Theory*. New York: Norton, 1988.

Kuhn, Thomas. "Scientists and Their Worldview." In *The Truth About the Truth: De-Confusing and Re-Constructing the Postmodern World*, edited by Walt Anderson, 189-198. A New Consciousness Reader. New York: Putnam, 1995.

Levick, Eddie. "It Takes Guts to Get Out of the Ruts." *Moment of Meditation*. http://www.mcba.com/Action/Devotion.nsf/a1 61246e35e1e46b86256449007474e6/50d7cf36 e212809f862567f6000e3798?OpenDocument.

Lewis, Ralph L., and Gregg Lewis. *Learning to Preach Like Jesus.* Westchester, Ill.: Crossway Books, 1989.

Loughlin, Gerard. *Telling God's Story: Bible, Church, and Narrative Theology*. New York: Cambridge University Press, 1996.

Luhrmann, T. M. *Of Two Minds: The Growing Disorder in American Psychiatry*. New York: Knopf, 2000.

Lynn, Elizabeth, and Barbara G. Wheeler. "Missing Connections: Public Perceptions of Theological Education and Religious Leadership." *Auburn Studies* 6 (September 1999): 1–15.

McNeal, Reggie. "What About Seminary?" In *Revolution in Leadership Training Apostles for Tomorrow's Church. Ministry for the Third Millennium*. Nashville, Tenn.: Abingdon Press, 1998.

Monk, Gerald. "How Narrative Therapy Works." In *Narrative Therapy in Practice: the Archaeology of Hope*, 7-31. San Francisco: Jossey-Bass Publishers, 1997.

Myers, William. *Research in Ministry: A Primer for the Doctor of Ministry Program*. Studies in Ministry and Parish Life. Chicago: Exploration Press, 2000.

Nichols, Michael, and Richard Schwartz. *Family Therapy: Concepts and Methods*. 5th ed. Boston: Allyn and Bacon, 2001.

Oden, Thomas C. *Pastoral Theology: Essentials of Ministry*. San Francisco: Harper & Row, 1982.

Parsons, Talcott. *The Social System*. New York London: The Free Press Collier-Macmillan Ltd., 1964.

_____, and Robert Freed Bales. *Family Socialization and Interaction Process*. Glencoe, Ill.: Free Press, 1954.

Pattison, Stephen. "Some Straw for the Bricks: A Basic Introduction to Theological Reflection." In *The Blackwell Reader in Pastoral and Practical Theology*, edited by James Woodward, Stephen Pattison, and John Patton, 135-145.. Malden, MA: Blackwell Publishers, 2000.

Pink, Daniel H. "Schools Out." In *Free Agent Nation How America's New Independent Workers Are Transforming the Way we Live*. New York: Warner Books, 2001.

Ricœr, Paul. *Time and Narrative*. Chicago: University of Chicago Press, 1984.

Robson, Colin. *Real World Research: A Resource for Social Scientists and Practitioner-Researchers*. Malden, MA: Blackwell Publishers, 2002.

Ruether, Rosemary Radford. *Disputed Questions: On Being a Christian. Journeys in Faith*. Nashville: Abingdon, 1982.

Satir, Virginia. *The New Peoplemaking*. Mountain View, CA: Science and Behavior Books, 1988.

Schaller, Lyle. "How Does the Culture Impact the Church? The Call to Customize." *Net Results* 5 (November/December 2000): 3–7.

Schreiter, Robert J. *Constructing Local Theologies*. Maryknoll, N.Y.: Orbis Books, 1985.

Stark, Rodney. *The Rise of Christianity: A Sociologist Reconsiders History*. Princeton, NJ: Princeton University Press, 1996.

Steere, David A. *Spiritual Presence in Psychotherapy: A Guide for Caregivers*. New York: Brunner/Mazel, 1997.

Stevens, Paul R., and Phil Collins. *The Equipping Pastor: A Systems Approach to Congregational Leadership.* Washington, DC: Alban Institute, 1993.

Sweet, Leonard I. *Eleven Genetic Gateways to Spiritual Awakening.* Nashville: Abingdon, 1998.

Sweet, Leonard I., Brian D. McLaren, and Jerry Haselmayer. *"A" Is for Abductive: The Language of the Emerging Church.* Grand Rapids, MI: Zondervan, 2003.

Thoreau, Henry David. *The Writings of Henry David Thoreau.* Edited by Bradford Torrey and F. B. Sanborn. New York: Houghton, Mifflin and Company, 1906.

Thurneysen, Eduard. *A Theology of Pastoral Care.* Richmond, VA: John Knox Press, 1962.

Winslade, John, and Alison Cotter. "Moving from Problem Solving to Narrative Approaches in Mediation." In *Narrative Therapy in Practice: the Archaeology of Hope*, 252-74. San Francisco: Jossey-Bass Publishers, 1997.

***

39682749R00086

Made in the USA
Lexington, KY
06 March 2015